"*After We're Gone* is unique in the way it addresses the agonizing issue of healthcare sponsorship. An awesome legacy is graciously recognized; transitions are carefully analyzed; visions of novel sponsorships with their core competencies are modestly suggested. Richly informative from broad experience; startlingly frank on problems institutional and individual, administrative and emotional; movingly insistent on the need to acknowledge and ritualize transition, to memorialize the old, release the grief, celebrate the new; aware that the next generation of sponsors must be grounded in the Gospel and a profound yet practical ecclesiology–this little book could serve as a stimulus for discussions across the whole spectrum, not only of Catholic healthcare but of education as well."

Walter J. Burghardt, SJ
Senior Fellow, Woodstock Theological Center
Washington, D.C.

"Kathryn Grant and Patricia Vandenberg are not strangers to the struggles and complexities of sponsorship. For the past twenty years, they have been leading thinkers and practitioners in this arena. Such experience enables them to write a book that is both conceptual and practical, challenging and encouraging. Congregational leaders, trustees, administrative staff, and interested diocesan leaders will find their historical overview and current analysis honest, informative and helpful. All who are responsible for planning and/or direction-setting will benefit from the expertise contained in this slender volume."

Helen Marie Burns, RSM
Co-Director, Kirtland Volunteer Action Center
Roscommon, Michigan

"The coauthors offer an honest and courageous assessment of the challenges facing sponsors of Catholic healthcare. They provide a thoughtful description of the evolution of religious congregational sponsorship, employing the analogy of the family-owned business to the demands of partnering with others. Emphasis is placed on the requisites for responsible decision making in ensuring the future healing ministry, the important stages of grieving and the necessity to ritualize the experience of loss. An important read for today's Catholic healthcare sponsor, this insightful commentary and personal reflection have wider implications for leaders of all ministries of the Church."

Most Rev. Joseph M. Sullivan, DD
Episcopal Vicar for Human Services
Diocese of Brooklyn
Brooklyn, New York

"*After We're Gone* brings clarity and challenge to the complex discussion of religious sponsorship. Honoring the U.S. Catholic heritage in education and healthcare ministries, the authors map a path of creative fidelity that will help assure its future. Religious sponsors and lay leaders alike will find this analysis honest, evocative and astute."

Evelyn Eaton Whitehead and James D. Whitehead
Whitehead Associates
Consultants in Education and Ministry
South Bend, Indiana

——————————— ⚙ ———————————

After WE'RE GONE:

CREATING SUSTAINABLE Sponsorship

MARY KATHRYN GRANT, PhD
SISTER PATRICIA VANDENBERG, CSC, MHA

After We're Gone: Creating Sustainable Sponsorship

ISBN 0-9668589-0-5

After We're Gone:

Creating Sustainable Sponsorship

Table of Contents

After WE'RE GONE:

CREATING SUSTAINABLE Sponsorship

Acknowledgments

We would like to thank those many persons who have contributed to our thinking on this critical subject, have challenged us, and have encouraged us to complete the writing in the midst of demands of our ministry. To attempt to name these individuals risks that we might overlook someone—nevertheless we would like to acknowledge:

- *Catherine O'Brien, CSC,* president of the Sisters of the Holy Cross, who first introduced the concept of the *community of committed persons*;

- *James Hendricks,* chair of the Holy Cross Health System Corporation Board of Directors, an esteemed leader in the *community of committed persons* that makes up the health system;

- *Jim* and *Evelyn Whitehead* who concurred with our concern that there be an articulated theology of sponsorship and then helped shape our language and conceptual framework;

- *Helen Marie Burns, RSM*, who for years chided "Why don't you write this down for the rest of us?" and then agreed to read and comment on the manuscript;

- *Jeremy Daigler, RSM,* who in responding to the Mercy Pathways Project poignantly posed the key question "What *will* happen *after we are gone?*";

- *Christa Hojlo, CSC,* whose support and vision in reading the signs of the times has encouraged this effort;

- *MSSC,* the "ole girls club" of Mission and Sponsorship, who so lovingly and generously endured, encouraged, and nurtured these ideas over the years;

- *Moni McIntyre* and *Heather MacKinnon, SSND,* who helped these ideas along during their long incubation;

- *Bishop Joseph M. Sullivan* who has been a trusted advisor and loyal friend and supporter of Catholic healthcare throughout the years;

- *Walter J. Burghardt, SJ,* whose writing and conversations have challenged our thinking and whose thoughtful and thorough reading sharpened and challenged the text;

- *Paul Marceau, Kathe Brunton* and *Louise Koselak* whose rigorous reviews and critical questions contributed to the final editing;

- *Jodi Garrett* whose excellent visual communications skills have guided the design and publication process; and

- all those unnamed persons whose lives have been an inspiration to us and who have journeyed with us in pursuit of a future for our ministries even greater than the past.

We are human beings;
for whom birth is a supremely welcome mystery,
the mystery of growing:
the mystery which happens only
and whenever we are faithful to ourselves.[1]

E. E. Cummings

INTRODUCTION

After We're Gone: Creating Sustainable Sponsorship

The title for this volume, "After We're Gone," was borrowed from a question raised by a sister-teacher in response to a questionnaire about the future of sponsored educational ministry. Her query touched deeply on a pressing matter facing religious congregations of women and men. She asked thoughtfully, "What will happen to our sponsored institutions *after we are gone?*" The *we* of the title is deliberately ambiguous: for some religiously sponsored organizations, this *we* refers to the congregation which founded and which continues to have canonical responsibility for the work. For other organizations, as will be described later in this volume, the *we* refers to the religious and laity who currently share responsibility for the ministry today.

As the twentieth century draws to a close, this is the critical question. What will become of sponsored works, and what must sponsorship become to assure the survival of the ministries of healthcare, education, and social services begun and, until recently, sponsored almost exclusively by religious congregations of women and men? In 1900, sisters staffed more than 3,800 parochial schools, 645 orphanages, 633 schools for girls, and more than 500 hospitals. By 1960, those numbers had grown to 12,455 schools and more than 800 hospitals staffed by 150,000 women religious.[2] By the last decade of the twentieth century, however, the numbers of women religious had declined sharply, and today there are fewer than 20,000 sisters in these institutions. The number of congregations sponsoring hospitals and educational facilities has likewise declined and will continue to decline.

Sisters opened schools and orphanages often within their convents to begin the care and education of young people, many of whom were from an immigrant population who had migrated from the same countries as the sisters themselves. Part of the motivation for launching educational ministry was the preservation of the faith, but there was also a strong urgency rooted in social justice to provide a better future for women by teaching them arts and humanities together with skills and trades. These motivations sustained sponsored educational ministry in the United States until the late 1960s and 1970s when forces within the congregations and in society irrevocably altered the face and the history of Catholic schools: current and future sister-teachers elected new ministries; financial constraints forced the closure or consolidation of many parish schools; and laity in large numbers began to staff and administer Catholic educational institutions.

The earliest form of healthcare ministry was a forerunner of home nursing in which sisters visited the sick and elderly in their own homes. When this was no longer feasible, primitive hospitals were established. The oldest continually operating hospital in the United States was begun by the Sisters of Mercy in Pittsburgh in an abandoned orchestra hall during a cholera epidemic. The sisters had found that ill sailors were thrown ashore from passing vessels in order to stop the spread of the disease aboard the ships. Abandoned to die, the sailors were first brought into the convent itself where the sisters nursed the dying. Later, as the numbers of ill grew and it was not safe to expose the other resident sisters to disease, a makeshift hospital was organized. Within a few decades, military nursing had its beginnings as sisters left their classrooms to nurse the wounded Civil War soldiers from both sides on the battlefields and on the *Red Rover*, the first hospital ship.

From these beginnings developed the most extensive private school system and the largest not-for-profit "system" of hospitals in the United States. From their earliest days, these sponsored institutional ministries resembled family businesses wherein distinctions between ownership, management and staff were blurred— if existent at all. Sponsorship was not a word in anyone's vocabulary until the late 1970s. At that time, Sister Concilia Moran, RSM, then administrator general of the Sisters of Mercy of the Union, brought the word into popular usage. In a circular letter to the congregation, Sister Concilia identified sponsorship with "projects, programs, and institutions for which the Sisters...are corporately responsible."[3]

Sister Concilia further defined sponsorship as "support of, influence on and responsibility for a project, program or institution which furthers the goals of the sponsoring group." She added, "Sponsorship further implies that the sponsoring group is publicly identified with the project, program or institution, and makes certain resources available to them."[4] Thus was launched a pursuit of probing more deeply the meaning of sponsorship which has continued for more than twenty years.

Until the 1970s, sponsorship (and all that it entailed) was taken for granted. The mere physical presence of sisters, often in large numbers, defined sponsorship as if it were a quantifiable reality. Critical questions from this period were: "How many sisters (brothers or priests) were necessary for sponsorship? Could the facility be sponsored by the congregation if there were no sisters in ministry? or in governance?" These very questions presage the question which this book addresses: What will happen to our sponsored works *after we are gone*? How can sustainable models of sponsorship be created while the founding sponsors are still strong and able to create a viable future?

This book features three elements: essays of a more didactic nature; personal reflections on the themes of the essays; and questions for personal or communal discussion and discernment. The authors have wrestled with these very questions for several decades in both education and healthcare settings. The essays detail the themes from the perspectives of both education and healthcare while the personal reflections are rooted in reflection by one of the authors on a lifelong healthcare ministry.

The book is written for both current and future sponsors, for executive leadership within these sponsored works, and for all those who serve with and are concerned about the future of these ministries. For current sponsors, it provides a vehicle to reflect on the changing nature of their sponsorship and the urgency to act while there is still time. For future sponsors, this volume will deepen their understanding of the awesome legacy they have inherited and inspire their full commitment to assure a future that is even stronger and greater than the past.

The first chapter outlines some of the major themes of the book and expands on the notion of the family business as a metaphor for congregationally sponsored ministries. It traces the emergence of institutional ministries from the early "mom and pop" shops through the current requirements of ministerial partnerships with lay collaborators. Paralleling the evolution of sponsorship is the introduction and development of a mission function in sponsored works. The congruence between the growing emphasis on sponsorship and the increasing importance of mission functions is detailed. This section concludes, as do all sections, with a personal reflection on the journey in ministry and sponsorship. Reflection questions follow.

The next section details the urgency for action as the "family business" model fades. It may appear to some that this urgency for action is grounded in pessimism. That is not its intention. It is intended to be a wake up call to both current sponsors and their successors, on the need, to act thoughtfully and carefully now. Or as someone recently quipped, "Any narrative about sponsorship should be titled, 'If I should die before you wake . . .'" Personal reflections and questions follow.

The third section deals with the necessity of acknowledging and ritualizing the transition: the loss of the old and the welcoming celebration of the new. In so doing, it paves the way for the final section which contains an approach to preparing the "next generation" of sponsors by identifying the core competencies needed for sponsorship. The inspiration for this chapter came from reflecting on a homily by Walter J. Burghardt, SJ. A personal reflection on this issue is shared, followed by questions.

The later sections of this volume move tentatively into the arena of a theology of sponsorship. The authors look at models of sponsorship—in the Church and in society— and endeavor to lay out an approach to developing such a theology. It is only a beginning and is rudimentary at best. Development of such a theology is imperative, however, if the next generation is to be grounded in the Gospel and in a solid ecclesiology. The authors believe that only through the creation of communities of persons dedicated to a common mission, mutual accountability, and commitment to fidelity to the spirit of the founders will there be sustainable models of sponsorship for the third millennium.

Mary Kathryn Grant and *Sister Patricia Vandenberg, CSC*
Advent 1998 • South Bend, Indiana

PART I

The Origins and Evolution of Contemporary Sponsorship

It is wise to continue the reflections begun some years ago about the Catholic identity of a[n] institution . . . Roles must be defined and the vision which once was only that of the religious must be shared by all. It is a complicated moment of [our] history . . ., but also a crucial one.[5]

Most Rev. Rembert G. Weakland, OSB
Archbishop of Milwaukee
1985

The Origins and Evolution of Contemporary Sponsorship[6]

Women and men religious in American institutional ministries, particularly Catholic education and healthcare ministries, have always embraced challenges. Since their earliest days, they have sought creative, innovative ways not only to preserve, but also to strengthen and ensure the future viability of service to the sick, the uneducated, the needy, children, the elderly, the poor—services which were organized and delivered through institutions or formal organizations. The earliest organizational form of these ministries best resembles that of a family business or a "mom and pop" shop. Over time that organizational model evolved into one of more formal sponsorship and ultimately to the actual institutionalization of sponsorship itself.

Today, however, one of the greatest threats to the future of these ministries lies within the very organization of these sponsored works: the post Vatican II emphasis on the unique charism or characteristics and culture of the sponsor and a desire to preserve these in the form of a family business. In this regard, three complex forces are at play during this last decade of the twentieth century: the deeply felt need for some congregations to continue to preserve their own unique identity and sponsorship; a reliance by some congregations on these sponsored works for their very self-identity and future as a religious institute; and, often, a dependence on the works themselves for financial support, most often through the salaries of members serving in the organizations and occasionally through sponsorship fees. As a result of this desire to preserve sponsorship as it is now exercised and experienced, current consolidation efforts, such as a variety of collaborative arrangements, cosponsorship and transfer of sponsorship, represent unique challenges to today's sponsors.

This first section will explore the origins of the current model of sponsorship and identify some of the threats this organizational structure poses to the future of education and healthcare ministries. The emergence and growing importance of sponsorship will be traced from the earliest and rudimentary recognition of the elements of sponsorship to the present need for new models of sustainable sponsorship.

For the purposes of this writing, *sponsorship* is defined as the canonical responsibility the sponsor (traditionally the religious congregation or diocese) has for the ministry which includes both the "ecclesiastical property," that is, property or goods used for the ministry, and the faithful oversight and administration of the works. Throughout this volume, family business is used as a metaphor to depict the relationship between the religious congregation/sponsor acting as the founding family and referring to the sponsored works as the family business. This metaphor will be discussed in greater detail in the next section of the book.

There are clearly limits to the usefulness of any metaphor or analogy. The image of a family business in this context serves as an organizing metaphor for religious congregations as sponsors. It also provides a helpful framework and language for naming the realities and tracing the developments, changes, and challenges of the continued evolution of sponsorship and the movement away from a family-like relationship to one which resembles more an alliance or partnership. Examining the life cycles of family businesses against the life cycles of organizations likewise offers a helpful conceptual framework for analysis and reflection.

THE BEGINNINGS

During the eighteenth and early nineteenth centuries, it was customary in American society to care for the ill in their homes; only the poor and homeless were cared for in "ill houses"—as the hospitals then were called. Members of religious congregations often brought the sick into their own convents for care and, when this was not possible, rented homes to shelter and care for them.

The impetus to establish Catholic hospitals came in part—according to the annals of religious congregations —during epidemics when the sick poor were not welcomed in the ill houses, and convents were not able to accommodate all those in need both in terms of space and for fear of endangering the lives of others in residence. Similar stories of schools being housed within the convents—either day schools or boarding schools in which the religious lived on the upper floors—abound in the history of religious congregations.

The further rapid growth of these organized ministries of health and education occurred as a result of the great influx of Catholic immigrants to American cities. Parishes established schools for the education and evangelization of their young and, on occasion, even founded hospitals in circumstances where Catholics were not welcomed in public hospitals. Undaunted and indefatigable, women and men religious in these early days creatively sought ways to minister—despite overwhelming odds.[7]

Sisters followed the Catholic immigrant populations across the United States, setting up primary schools, academies, normal schools and colleges. Sometimes acting on their own and at other times responding to the persistent pleas of bishops and other clergy, women and men religious ultimately created one of the greatest legacies of the American Church: the Roman Catholic school system. These spontaneous and informal ministries eventually became more formally organized works and were viewed, more and more, as belonging to or sponsored by various congregations. The notion of sponsorship was created to name the reality of this intimate relationship between the congregation and its schools and healthcare institutions.

HISTORICAL PERSPECTIVES

In recent time, six distinct periods in the development and evolution of religiously sponsored ministries can be identified: pre-1960s, or before Vatican II; the post-Vatican II decades—the 1960s, 1970s, 1980s, 1990s; and 2000 and beyond. Focusing on four elements—governance, management, sponsorship, and organization or structural relationships—reveals emerging trends. (See Figure 1.) Each of these decades has been marked with significant and often dramatic changes in the Church, the evolution of religious life in the United States, and the sociopolitical environment of healthcare and education.

Four Waves of Sponsorship

It is helpful, at this point, to identify four waves or developments in the evolution of sponsorship. These waves correlate to the continuing participation of the "family" or the congregation in the ministry. (See Figure 2.) The first wave, briefly described, can be classified as the "family business" wave; the second wave might be likened to a "franchise" in which the family spells out its require-ments and expectations as participation in the works

Figure 1

EVOLUTION OF SPONSORSHIP

PERIOD	GOVERNANCE	MANAGEMENT	SPONSORSHIP	ORGANIZATION
Pre-1960	Local superior and council	Local superior as CEO	Not clearly defined; frequently identified with number of religious	Stand-alone, independent healthcare facilities; school "systems" within congregations
1960s	All-religious boards; lay advisory hospital boards; school boards	Predominantly religious, few laypersons; appointment by the religious congregation's leadership	Beginning of formal definition: tied to appointments of CEOs and boards; still synonymous with numerical presence	Beginnings of centralized services for healthcare facilities, generally through motherhouse offices—similar to education
1970s	Formal boards— religious and laity serving together	Approximately 50% lay hospital CEOs; growing numbers of lay principals, presidents	Continued search for definition; influence role emerging	Healthcare systems developing, generally based within single congregation; withdrawal from congregational sponsorship of schools
1980s	Boards fully integrated: lay and religious	Copartnership of religious and laity serving in executive leadership	Searching for the most effective locus: management or governance	Alliances, networks and multi-congregation arrangements; health systems; college university consortia
1990s	Professional boards, some paid members in health (generally religious)	Professional management; full incorporation of laity into ministry	Two models: lay and religious congregation	Mega health systems regionally or nationally; fully integrated systems; college mergers or cosponsorships
2000	True governing boards; in healthcare with fiduciary responsibilities for integrated health system	Little change: professional managers in both hospitals and in educational administration	Increasingly more models of lay sponsorship; few solely religiously sponsored organizations	Continued consolidation in health and education ministries; in healthcare with emphasis on critical mass at regional level

Figure 2

THE EVOLUTIONARY WAVES OF SPONSORSHIP

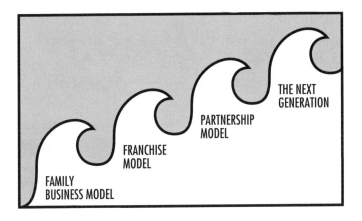

expands beyond congregational members. This expansion is not unlike the manner in which a franchised business articulates the terms and conditions of maintaining the franchise. The third wave resembles a partnership in which family and non-family members actively participate in the mission and operations of the ministry/business. The fourth wave moves beyond congregational sponsorship to lay sponsorship and may take the form of public or private juridic person or private associations of the Christian faithful. This model will be discussed in greater detail later in the book.

In the first wave of the evolution, family members predominate in management and governance roles giving rise to the metaphor of the family-run business. As there were fewer family members to manage and govern schools, colleges, universities and healthcare facilities, lay persons were brought in while the "family" set standards for mission fulfillment, quality, critical components of operations and, in some instances, culture as well, similar to a franchise in other businesses. As comfort and experience grew with non-family members assuming a more active and integral role in these ministries, the "franchise" model began to evolve into one resembling more of a partnership, in a nonlegal sense. In this third wave, identified as partnership, trusted laity were enabled to participate in the actual articulation of and accountability for mission and values. Finally, lay sponsors may emerge as the surviving mode of sponsorship in the next century.

Hence the image of four waves captures the spirit of the evolution from the model of family business to a franchise model and then to partnership during the time when the family or the religious congregation maintained active roles and participation in the ministry. In the section which follows, the consequences of the family no longer being able to sustain a significant role and participation in the ministry will be discussed more fully. It should be observed, however, that each sponsor has moved or will move through the waves of evolution as described above. The progress through this evolution is dependent on a number of factors. The number of members continuing to serve in institutional ministries and the theological perspective and personal comfort of the sponsor regarding lay partnership are among the most determinative.

The First Wave: The Family Business

The overlapping of roles and lack of differentiation in responsibilities between the convent and the sponsored work may be captured somewhat tongue in cheek as "keys, kitchen privileges, and privileged information." (See Figure 3.) *Keys* symbolize the unrestricted access members of the sponsoring group had to all areas of the facility, including access to equipment and supplies: offices, auditoriums, conference rooms, faculty lounges—congregational members were able to access these whenever they so desired. They also had access to positions within the institutions sponsored by their congregations, a phenomenon discussed in greater detail in the next section.

Figure 3

SYMBOLS OF THE FAMILY OWNERSHIP

SYMBOLS OF FAMILY OWNERSHIP	ATTRIBUTES
Keys	• Access to services, personnel, equipment • Unlimited use of facility for "family" affairs, congregational meetings
Kitchen Privileges	• Employment "perks" and benefits not available to others • Housing and transportation options
Privileged Information	• "Family members" with access to decisions and decision makers

The universal respect personnel in the organizations had for the religious who served there led to the second feature: *kitchen privileges*. Privileges, for example, as special meals for feast days or other special days provided by the kitchen or prepared by the religious themselves in the institutional kitchens. Basically "kitchen privileges" refers to those expectations above and beyond the normal or customary expectations of those who serve in the organization. Moreover, it was not uncommon for members of the sponsoring congregation to be exempt from personnel policies, performance review, and the like.

Finally, there was *privileged information*. When the convent superior met with the assembled community, she generally shared information on two fronts—first, regarding the operations of the convent household and, then, whatever had been discussed by the local superior and her council and decided about the sponsored works. Family members were in the mainstream of information and decision making. Hence, the spirit of these earlier times could be captured in "keys, kitchen privileges, and privileged information." No criticism of these practices is intended in this discussion, only a naming of the certain expectations and privileges available to family members within a family business.

The Second Wave: The Franchise Model

The second wave of sponsorship, characterized by attributes which resemble those of a franchise, occurred after Vatican II and the sweeping social changes in American society in the 1960s and 1970s. These decades witnessed major social movements in society and consequently impacted the operation of a family business model of sponsorship. Considerable numbers of individuals in religious congregations opted out of institutional ministries in favor of more hands-on or social justice ministries; doors to whole new avenues of service opened up as a result of the Sister Formation Movement, begun in the 1950s, which urged the completion of educational preparation and occasioned an openness to new areas of study such as law, medicine and social work. By the 1970s the decline in the number of religious prepared for, or accepting roles in, management or institutional leadership necessitated the appointment of lay administrators who often were selected by the religious congregation's leadership. This situation coupled with the changes occasioned by Vatican II encouraged greater involvement of the laity in all aspects of the apostolic mission of the Church, including healthcare and education.

It would be a serious misperception to attribute these changes solely to the decline in the actual number of active religious and in the number of religious who chose to serve in the institutional ministry, particularly in management. Many of these changes were in response to Vatican II and a deeper and increased understanding of the laity's integral role in the Church's life and mission. Recognizing a call to service as part of one's baptismal commitment, many generous and dedicated laypersons elected to work in religiously sponsored institutions— schools, colleges and healthcare facilities—to assume leadership and governance and ultimately sponsorship roles.

The Emergence of Governance:
Transition to the Third and Fourth Waves

Governance was another emerging critical function as these sponsored works matured and evolved through the three waves. In the case of healthcare, the civil courts began to define a fiduciary role on hospital boards. Although these early ministries did not have true governing boards, a quasi-governance role was exercised by the leadership of the local convents. Later, when a more formal governance structure emerged, the trustees of religiously sponsored institutions were generally religious appointed by the superior of the sponsoring congregation. At the same time, lay advisory boards increased in number and influence, while most institutions were independent, stand-alone facilities.

During these same decades of the '60s and '70s, sponsorship of educational institutions was more precisely defined or redefined with the resultant transfer of responsibility for the administration, staffing, and financing of parish schools back to the parishes themselves. Over time this led to the formation of centralized diocesan school systems and the strengthening of diocesan school boards. These developments, however welcomed, were portents of greater changes which occasioned loss and a need for ritualizing and grieving the changes. Not infrequently the cries, "These used to be our schools (or hospitals) . . ." or "They don't tell us anything anymore . . . " were heard.

As management and governance became more formalized, more complex and formal channels of decision making and dissemination of information were necessarily created. These changes meant the religious in the sponsored work often had to await formal communications and in some cases to relinquish their unlimited access to the facility. Eventually religious had to apply for positions in the institutions through more formal personnel procedures; eventually they were required to compete with non-family members for positions. As might be assumed, these developments had profound effect on the family and on the family business, as well as on relationships within the business between family and non-family members.

Increased lay involvement has been a universal phenomenon in Catholic ministry. Religious congregations of necessity have had to grapple with new issues such as role clarification and lay leadership formation and to come to terms with the demands of sponsoring schools, colleges, and universities as well as large and complex healthcare systems. In the face of a turbulent environment, the changing requirements in governance and management and the increasing need to define sponsorship and stewardship commitments, new roles and new players emerged with responsibilities for these ministries, ultimately creating the third wave.

The Third Wave: Partnership

The changing face of healthcare compounds the evolving sponsorship challenges. Nationally, the healthcare world of the 1970s increased attention to the business aspects of operating complex organizations. Divestiture, selling or closing of smaller or more remote facilities, and the beginnings of a movement toward establishing or strengthening corporate offices and centralized consulting services under the religious congregation's aegis gathered momentum. These initial efforts generally were focused on the healthcare facilities sponsored by the particular congregation. Since the mid- 1970s, lay appointments have accelerated rapidly, and so much so that by 1979 almost half the administrators of Catholic hospitals were not members of the sponsoring congregation.

The 1980s brought additional change along the directions begun in the 1970s: greater lay involvement; greater emphasis on the need to integrate those who minister with the religious congregation's members; the need for leadership formation; and, perhaps more significantly, a growing willingness on the part of religious congregations with a few facilities to seek modes of collaboration with other religious sponsors— turning the tide from the growing numbers of divestitures to linkages among congregations. In some ways this trend toward linkages parallels both new and revitalized efforts to impart the unique culture or charism of the sponsors and the gradual incorporation and growing collaboration of the laity in ministry.

Consistent with the trends discussed earlier, the 1990s have witnessed new models of organization: ministries sponsored by several religious congregations and ministries organized along regional lines and the beginnings of lay-sponsored ministries. Governing boards have begun to take the place of volunteer boards at corporate levels. Colleges and universities have also moved more clearly in the direction of lay sponsorship, sometimes inadvertently or without formal processes, the shift having occurred in earlier decades. The day of the professional trustee has been predicted and already some religious serve together with laypersons as professional trustees in corporate ministries.

With these major changes occurring during the last decades, a new and more burning question appeared: Where to position the members of the family who were able and interested in active roles in the ministry? This question, arising as the family business model recedes from the picture, shapes a crucial decision for congregations today regarding the locus of influence: governance or management. A number of follow-up questions also surface: Where to channel the energy of the congregational members? How to safeguard the heritage and legacy of so many years of service in ministry? Where to look for the next generation of sponsors?

Toward the Fourth Wave

In the fourth wave in which the ultimate move is to a new juridic person as sponsor, in true evolutionary manner elements of the earlier waves endure. A fuller discussion of this movement follows in the later sections of this book. However, it is important to note that some enduring developments are evident from earlier waves.

A pivotal role began to emerge in these changing times: the establishment of a function within the organization charged first with mission and later with sponsorship responsibilities. This role in effect becomes the link between the sponsoring congregation and the corporation or institutional ministry. In the absence of large numbers of members of sponsoring congregations to serve in either governance or management positions and with the increasing complexity of the environment, the responsibilities of mission and sponsorship are viewed alternately as interpreter of the congregation's mission and as liaison between corporation and congregation and between corporation and individual facilities.

The Emergence of Mission Roles

Not unlike the four waves of sponsorship evolution, there have been distinct developments in the evolution of the mission and sponsorship role in institutional ministries. (See Figure 4.) The early experience of this role was that of the appointment of a member of the sponsoring congregation who could promote mission awareness and organize special celebrations to commemorate the founding, the patron or some other feast or occasion with special meaning to the organization or the congregation. This period may be labeled the "mascot" phase, a phrase used frequently by mission leaders to describe their own experience of the role: the mission leader (sponsorship was not linked with mission initially) as an animating force explaining and helping to pass on the congregation's heritage, philosophy and unique culture. Persons charged with mission responsibilities were often recruited from other ministries and lacked critical technical and practical experience. They often struggled with the complexities of organizational life in the new setting.

Figure 4

THE EVOLUTION OF MISSION ROLES

IMAGE	ATTRIBUTES
Mascot	• Specialized activities • Awareness building • Mission Statements
Mentor	• Incorporation into human resources • Behavioral norms for mission performance • Mission education
Mainstream	• Integration with strategic planning • Norms for mission integration • Mission Accountability

During the '70s, following the introduction of mission roles in many organizations, frustration was expressed on both sides. Mission leaders often expressed feelings of being inadequately prepared for their roles, marginalized, and without colleagues with whom to network. On the other hand, the management of the organizations confessed to confusion about how best to utilize the skills and maximize the contributions this person could make. Only recently has there been serious discussion of the core competencies required for this role, notwithstanding the deeper question of whether or not the mission person had to be a member of the family, i.e. the religious congregation sponsoring the ministry/family business.

Not long after the creation of this position, an awareness deepened that this role had to become more central and more integral to the life and operation of the organization. This insight led to the early attempts to professionalize the role and spawned the second phase in the development of mission responsibility in which mission and human resource leaders linked arms to develop mission education programs. During this phase, mission integration took on more critical dimensions and demands. Working initially with recruitment, selection, and orientation, mission and human resource personnel sought to assure that those individuals working within the organization thoroughly imbued the values and vision of the sponsors. Behavioral indicators of mission fulfillment or mission integration

total educational or healthcare ministry, has far-reaching ramifications.

The demands of ministering to God's people through sponsored institutions require courage, generosity, fidelity, and a vision of the Church's mission. Barriers to the fullness of this ministry can come from many sources, internal and external. The same spirit that led women and men religious to begin new works, to establish new facilities, and to launch new ministries flourishes in the Church today. The charism of each religious congregation is from one Spirit, a gift to be given, to be used, to be spent. It is an evolving gifting to and for the Church. Ultimately, this post-conciliar age is witnessing the emergence of new spiritual endowments, of new corporate forms, with potentially stronger, more vital and viable ministries. In this time, congregations must re-vision, reassert, and celebrate that which unites them rather than that which sets them apart.

The times demand a more radical stance: a stance of community of persons, of congregations united to bring about the continued transformation of society, to bring about the reign of God. In her book, *Wrestling with God,* Barbara Fiand passionately asserts that congregational protectionism cannot have a place in a world called to radical transformation. The legacy of many religious congregations is a strong and vital Catholic ministry in education and healthcare. Their challenge is to enhance and to pass on that ministry, to use their charisms for the Church today and tomorrow.

Reflections on Ministry and Sponsorship: From the Bedside to the Boardroom

These reflections have been written by one of the authors, Sister Patricia Vandenberg, CSC, a Sister of the Holy Cross, who serves as the president of her congregation's health system. She comments on her own growth in understanding of and appreciation for what it means for a congregation to discern its commitment to sponsorship over the years.

I left New York in 1971 as a registered nurse with a bachelor's degree and a keen desire to serve the sick as a religious. I journeyed to South Bend, Indiana, to enter the Congregation of the Sisters of the Holy Cross. I returned to New York in 1990, to Wall Street to be exact, as president of one of the country's largest not-for-profit Catholic health systems to discuss the credit rating of the corporation and multimillion dollar debt issue needed to implement our system's strategic plan and fulfill our mission. I have been on a journey for these past twenty-seven years—a journey into the meaning and the mystery of sponsorship.

Returning from New York, I reflected on my first trip to South Bend. I realized that that original 600-mile trek began a journey from the bedside to the boardroom as I pondered and gradually learned the meaning and the challenges of ministering in works sponsored by a religious congregation during the last decade of the twentieth century. That journey, begun more than twenty-five years ago as a bedside nurse, initially revolved around my pursuit, first of professional excellence, then of ministry, and later of sponsorship.

This journey has brought me, today, to head a national health system where I can influence 19,000 employees, 6,000 physicians, and hundreds of volunteers and trustees who share the mission. My personal pursuit of ministry—from the bedside to the boardroom—was marked by many learnings: learnings about what mission means personally and what sponsorship must mean corporately.

There are unique aspects of my story, but our common story is written with many of the same experiences. As a teenager growing up in New York City, I realized I wanted to be a nurse. I thought I would apply to two schools, two diploma schools of nursing. That was the norm in those days. As it turned out, I was accepted at Roosevelt Hospital School of Nursing, and I was excited about the opportunities there, and so I went to pursue my nursing education in a community, nonsectarian, not-for-profit hospital environment.

What did I learn at the Roosevelt Hospital School of Nursing? Our faculty taught us that excellent nursing practice has two components—a caring, compassionate response to our patients and a deep commitment to professionalism and lifelong learning. I was exposed to some of the best medicine the world had to offer and also some of the worst physical facilities and scarcity of resources one might imagine. Since the Roosevelt Hospital was a community, nonsectarian hospital, the notion of nursing as a service was not one that was conveyed to us in religious terms. But by the time I graduated from Roosevelt, I had formed my own sense of mission and ministry; something that each of us must do personally. I had yet to learn about sponsorship. My journey had really just begun.

When I graduated from the Roosevelt Hospital, I pursued my BSN at Hunter College, which is part of the City University of New York. During my initial years in nursing, I had the opportunity to help open a cardiac care unit and to be part of the team that launched an open heart surgery program. Both of those initiatives constituted a response to the community's health needs. It was an exciting experience to be on the wave of innovation, to be on the leading edge of new medical developments, the implementation of new technologies, and the formation of new understandings of nursing care and community service.

In the summer of 1971, I left New York City and went to Cairo, Illinois, to spend the summer taking care of patients at Saint Mary's Hospital. I had been accepted into the Congregation of the Sisters of the Holy Cross. In light of the nursing shortage in Cairo, I was asked to volunteer for the summer at Saint Mary's. It was a fascinating experience to leave the high tech, intensive care environment in New York City and to step off a Greyhound bus into the marsh of Cairo, Illinois, in the heat of the summer. I felt that I was stepping back in time as I walked into that rural hospital setting. It was a profound experience to walk into one of the hospitals sponsored by the Sisters of the Holy Cross that dated back to the time of the Civil War and to realize that, ultimately, I was stepping into a world of sponsored health ministry that would define my very future.

Several years later, the congregation elected to withdraw its sponsorship of Saint Mary's Hospital. We had been there since the time of the Civil War. The hospital stayed open, but it became a community hospital with no religious affiliation. The congregation had withdrawn its sponsorship because we could not assure excellence in the delivery of health services in that community. My confidence in the depth of commitment of the Sisters of the Holy Cross to excellence in ministry was established and my understanding of some of the ramifications of sponsorship had begun to take shape. These two themes were to be intimately intertwined thereafter.

During the intervening years I served in several of my congregation's healthcare facilities in various capacities—

as nurse, as supervisor, as administrator, as trustee, and finally as president of the national health system itself. Throughout these years, my understanding and commitment to mission and ministry have deepened. I have stood in awe at the dedication and perseverance of members of the congregation to this ministry *per multos annos*. I have watched our lay colleagues become true partners in ministry: in embracing the mission with integrity and commitment, in practicing discernment in important decision making circumstances, in striving for excellence, and ever and ever greater stewardship of scarce and valued resources. And the journey continues. Its next leg for us has to be partnership in sponsorship as well as ministry.

As our congregation's human resources age and diminish, the search for news ways to continue sponsorship begins. Through years of consistent and progressive leadership formation and development in our system, we today have partners in ministry committed to the mission and prepared to move into the next century. Where we now need to direct our attention and effort is to the identification and development of partners in sponsorship: lay partners who will one day be the sponsors.

With the combined wisdom of the bedside and the boardroom, it seems apparent that in order for the ministry to have integrity in the future, it must be rooted in the Gospel and in a commitment to the ministry of governance as well as compassionate service. It is a rhythm of holding on and letting go, of expanding our vision and developing new skills and competencies. Today, as the CEO of a large health system, as a nurse and as a Sister of the Holy Cross, I sense we must be willing to trod new paths to secure a Catholic healthcare presence in the next century.

PART I

Questions for Personal or Group Reflection

- What has been my personal journey in mission? in sponsorship?

- The metaphors of keys, kitchen privileges, and privileged information are used to describe the family business model of relationship between members of the sponsoring body and its institutions. Do these images fit our experience? How?

- To what extent do we still operate in the mode of a "family business?" What reinforces this mode or is it just a continuation of the past? To what extent have we moved into the franchise model? Into the partnership model?

- How has the mission role evolved in our sponsored works?

- How firmly embedded is it in human resource activities?

- Has it reached the maturity of integration with planning? Does it have components of sponsorship? Should it? If so, how can this next level be attained?

PART II

The Transition of Sponsorship

We could be discouraged and lose heart...
We are older, our ranks are fewer...
but we are people of hope
and we await the harvest of fidelity....

A Holy Cross priest
on the eve of Jubilee 1998
Celebrations of Religious Profession

THE TRANSITION OF SPONSORSHIP:
THE FAMILY BUSINESS AND THE BUSINESS OF FAMILY

In a poem titled "Faith," David Whyte describes faith and faithfulness in a metaphor of the moon. The poet uses the expression "faithful in its fading" to describe the waning of the moon at the end of its cycle. Continuing to shed its illumination even as it passes from fullness, the moon moving throughout its cycle from new moon to full moon to the final absence of the moon becomes a fitting metaphor for fidelity. Not unlike these patterns of the moon, organizations, including family businesses, have discernible patterns. The ultimate challenge is to be faithful through all the phases.

In many ways this notion of being "faithful in the fading" can be applied to religiously sponsored ministries—healthcare and education, in particular—at this time of tremendous change or paradigm shift. Founded as they were by religious congregations and initially staffed, managed, and later governed by members of these same congregations, education and healthcare ministries today face declining numbers of members able, or in some cases interested, in continuing to accept the responsibilities of what we now call sponsorship. How then is fidelity, being faithful in the fading, to be exercised in these situations? How can this fading be named and addressed and, at the same time, the legacy and heritage of the founding family be cherished, preserved, and passed on?

Ironically, there were considerably more family members available, competent and willing to serve in institutional ministries, or the family business, during earlier times when there seemed to be less complexity to these ministries. While this judgment is ultimately subjective in its appreciation of complexity, there can be no quarrel with the fact that there were more religious active in institutional ministries, in all roles from administration to large numbers of staff positions, in earlier times.

Figure 5

PARTICIPATION AND COMPLEXITY SINCE THE 1960s

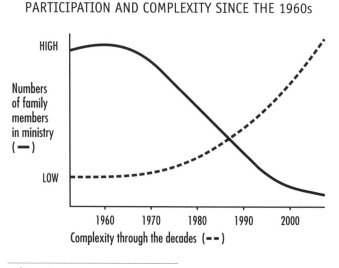

The similarities between religiously sponsored ministries and family businesses when comparing and contrasting some of the dynamics, dilemmas, and unique challenges associated with organizations whose governance, management, and work force come primarily from a common family or congregational base can be amply documented. The discussion that follows will address the particular discernment faced by these "family businesses" as the reserves of the family diminish in terms of numbers while changes and challenges in the external environment grow exponentially. Thus, pressures from within and without assail the ministry, the family business. The urgent question then is: How will congregations deal with diminished resources while remaining "faithful in the fading" as they move through the evolution of sponsorship? In examining these issues, learnings will be drawn from the growing body of research on family businesses and applied to religiously sponsored ministries, their family businesses.

This movement assumes the need for religious congregations to name, address, and deal with the reality that in the foreseeable future sponsorship of their ministries will, of necessity, be altered. The alterations will be through greater inclusion of non-family members in the very sponsorship and governance of the organizations or through merger, acquisition, affiliation, and possibly divestiture or closure. In other words, it appears inevitable that sponsorship, as it is has been exercised historically, has considerably changed. These changes mirror those faced by family businesses in transition. By drawing learnings from studies and findings of family businesses, today's sponsors can face the human dimensions and costs of these changes and exercise their characteristic fidelity in this time of fading.

Two recent studies of family businesses discuss the human dilemmas in the family firm, examining these matters from the vantage points of research and case studies. There are many applications of these findings to sponsored works, and much can be learned from them about how to handle the transitions that religiously sponsored ministries are currently facing. This section will draw especially from recent works by Manfred Kets de Vries, *Family Business: Human Dilemmas in the Family Firm,* and Kelin E. Gersick et al., *Generation to Generation: Life Cycles of the Family Business,* and apply their insights to the situation of contemporary sponsorship. This analysis and application in turn will shed light on the matters that need to be addressed by congregational sponsors and members, as well as with colleagues in ministry.

A most helpful framework for conceptualizing this comparison of religiously sponsored ministries to family business may be found in Gersick's work. He describes a three-circle model of family businesses in which ownership, family membership, and the business inter-sect. Through the overlapping of the circles, seven roles are identified (Figure 6):

Figure 6

THREE CIRCLES OF FAMILY BUSINESS[10]

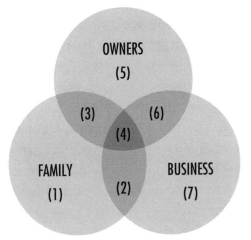

(Taguiri and Davis, 1982, 1996)

- Family members (1)
- Family members employed in the business (2)
- Family members with ownership responsibilities (3)
- Family members with ownership responsibilities, employed in the business (4)
- Owners who are neither family members nor employees (5)
- Owners who are employees but not family members (6)
- Employees who are neither family members nor owners (7)

Distinctions among these several roles may be most helpful particularly during this time of transition in understanding and sorting out the roles of members of the congregation, individuals charged with sponsorship responsibilities, and those individuals who serve in the sponsored works. A listing similar to that applied to the family business may be generated for religiously sponsored works. (See Figure 7.)

Members of the congregation at large (1) may identify with and support the family business, but not serve in any capacity in the business for a variety of reasons. On the one hand, members of the congregation who serve in the family business (2) may experience a sense of loss as fewer and fewer members of the family are able or available either to join or follow them. The sense of loss symbolized by no longer having keys, kitchen privileges, nor privileged information may capture their experience with the business.

On the other hand, sponsors and employees (5, 6, 7) who are not family members may have the experience of "outsiders," interlopers in the family business. As the complexity of sponsorship grows and the next generation of sponsors with the requisite competencies are appointed, the separation of the family from the business likewise increases.

These distinctions in roles may prove helpful in recognizing the range of feelings among participants as the paradigm shifts from family to non-family, and affected parties remain deeply committed to fidelity to the vision and values of the family business. The process of continually clarifying roles and responsibilities is a critical one, particularly during periods of transition and dramatic change.

Figure 7

THREE CIRCLES APPLIED TO SPONSORSHIP

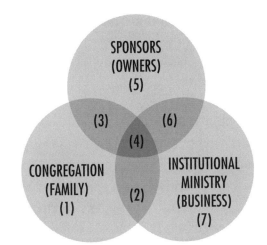

- Members of the congregation at large (1)
- Members of the congregation who serve in the sponsored works (2)
- Members of the congregation with sponsorship responsibilities (3)
- Members of the congregation in all three roles: sponsor, employee, member of the family/ the congregation (4)
- Sponsors from outside the congregation (5)
- Sponsors from outside the congregation who serve in the sponsored works (6)
- Employees (7)

THE CONTEXT

Expanding on the analogy of the family business, four contextual areas will be addressed: mission and vision, culture, leadership, and personnel matters. While each of these four areas has obvious positive attributes, each also has a negative or shadow side. The discussion that follows will describe both the positive and negative aspects of each of these four dimensions in relation to the family business of religious congregations.

Mission and Vision

The mission and vision of the family business—whether the family be a human family or a congregation—are extraordinarily compelling and sustaining. Embracing and endorsing the family's mission are predominant characteristics and critical success factors in most family businesses. Stories of the founders, often legendary in nature, abound and serve to keep alive this central or initial inspiration. Additionally, continuity of the mission and vision is assured through committed stakeholders—family and congregational members—who through blood or community ties carry on the vision of the founders constantly and faithfully. The mission of the family business often gives meaning and self-definition to the family and to its individual members.

Strong bonds among family members are established and sustained during the years of the existence of the company or ministry. Induction into the family business often occurs early in one's life, and expectations are placed on younger family members to assume responsibilities later for contributing to the family enterprise. Gatherings of the family or religious community keep its mission and vision alive and before the eyes of the members.

Celebrations and anniversaries mark significant milestones and achievements. On occasion these activities have led to over-identification of the family with the business—the congregation with its ministries—a topic addressed later in this volume.

Just as the mission and vision can be a principal source of strength, of unity and the creation of value, they can also be divisive, conflictive or competitive. Personal appropriation of the mission by the family can inadvertently create an "us" and "them" mentality, a caste system of insiders and outsiders. Mission, ironically, can also become a competitive force within the family. A healthcare mission may be viewed as competitive with an education mission, competing as it were, for personnel, the attention of leadership, visibility, and recognition among family/community members.

When clung to tenaciously, the mission can also be an impediment to growth and collaboration. Two circumstances may prevail: a confusion of the charism of the congregation with its ministries and a perceived need to preserve the one in order to assure the future viability of the other. The mission and charism of the sponsor are not one and the same with the mission of the institutional works. This fusion of identities and missions can lead to problems down the road for both the congregation and the ministry. When a congregation's mission, vision, or charism must be sustained or preserved at all costs, whether a result of the identification of the charism of the congregation and its ministry or the desire to preserve the unique charism expressed in the ministry itself, receptivity to discernment about collaboration is significantly diminished. This negative aspect of mission may be found in congregations that believe it is essential to preserve intact their own unique charism—no matter what. Preservation of the unique mission of a congregation can erode the vitality of the overall mission of healthcare and education.

Finally, it should be observed that there has been a history of competition between and among religious congregations as manifested in competition for vocations, for students and patients, teachers and physicians. These competitive feelings have long lives and often engender strong and deep responses from congregation members and lay partners.

Culture

Culture in a family business is basically established and maintained by the family and touches most aspects of both the organization and the family. Rituals, symbols, methods of doing things are long standing and often unchanging—and unchangeable. Culture itself is also a source of great pride and generates a sense of fulfillment among the members. Through culture, history and heritage are preserved and passed on from generation to generation. Not unlike the negative side of mission and vision, however, culture can be isolating and stifling. Expression of culture such as names, rituals, symbols and the like can be possessively retained.

The family name is time-honored and sacred. It is not uncommon in business today to extol the advantages of "branding," that is, using the same name and logo throughout a company, trading on the reputation of the family and the public recognition and status conveyed by the very use of the name itself. This same phenomenon occurs in religiously sponsored ministries: Jesuit colleges, Mercy hospitals, Carmelite nursing homes, Daughters of Charity orphanages, Christian Brothers secondary schools, Franciscan retreat centers—to cite but a few examples of "branding"— whether intentional or not.

The mere mention of the name of a congregation often conjures up an aspect of its charism that carries with it certain expectations, memories, connections. This is "branding" in its oldest and truest sense, and branding, in turn, reinforces the culture of the family business. The organization's name is a public symbol of its identity. Strong emotional attachment to the name and logo can lead to unreasonable requirements for retention of the same. Similarly, time-honored traditions and customs are neither easily abandoned nor modified or suspended.

Giving up or losing one's name or one's logo—however good the reasons or end result—presents a potentially traumatic experience of loss. One needs only to think of the movement for women to retain their maiden names and therefore symbolically retain their own identity in a marriage to know how deeply this need is felt.

Possessiveness of symbols and rituals can also present a challenge to be addressed in the face of growing collaborative initiatives. The recent wave of consolidation among Catholic healthcare sponsors has led to the relinquishing of "brand" names and the creation of more neutral, generic names, in order to signal the creation of something new—but it has also occasioned the loss of long-standing public identification. Mergers, affiliations, or other types of consolidations in which a new or blended name and a new identity is created require appropriate ritualization and grieving the loss of the former name, logo or public identification.

Strong identification of family members with the business is also characteristic of such enterprises. This identification sustains a strong culture, sometimes making it difficult for a family or congregational member to work outside the family business. It is not uncommon for members of the congregation, often unconsciously, to make those who do not work inside the family business feel guilty for abandoning their place in the business. Often there is the additional expectation that they "will return home" and assume their rightful role in the governance, management or operations of the business/ministry.

Leadership

Someone who has not experienced the challenge of shouldering the mantle of responsibility for a family business, whether at a local or corporate level, cannot fully appreciate what this leadership responsibility means and how weighty it can be. Pressures to assume the role in the first place, to meet the expectations of both the family and the business, and to be true to oneself impact individuals in leadership in a variety of ways. This pressure over time can be debilitating.

Unrealistic and heavy expectations come from both sources: the family and the business. In the case of a member of a religious congregation, these expectations can often be contradictory and irreconcilable. If the religious is "too businesslike," members of the congregation often express disappointment in them and devalue or disparage their role in the ministry. On the other hand, if the individual is not businesslike enough or "too religious," the business can suffer and professional colleagues can disparage their role.

Thus, in the extreme, this can become a virtual no-win situation. Too much attention to the demands of the business renders the individual religious with little time, energy, or ability to contribute to the business of the family itself, the congregation. Missing community events, not being able to serve on committees and task forces, needing to live alone because of the demands of the position, any of these factors can result in one being judged not faithful to one's primary commitment, being "married to one's job" or, worse, not "being a good religious."

Additionally, the interconnectedness of and the bonds between members of the religious congregation can create the same problems as occur between siblings within a family business. Family members often express disappointment in the persons themselves or their decisions which, in turn, can create inner conflict and turmoil for the persons called on to run the family business. They are often expected to be or do so much more. These unrealistic expectations, spoken or unspoken, can sap one's energy. Even worse, sibling rivalry can and does exist, sometimes covertly. Members of the congregation may become envious of the status, the prominence, or the visibility of the person in a leadership role in the family business.

Another major challenge to the leader who is a member of the sponsoring congregation arises when other forces converge: when the "foremothers" or matriarchs of the family business move into retirement or die and there are no younger members of the family to take over the leadership of the business. Described in the literature as the departing of both the parents and the offspring, this phenomenon is all too common in religiously sponsored ministries and can lead to an even deeper feeling of aloneness or abandonment within the leader. When the mentors or matriarchs are no longer active in the ministry and there is no one behind the leader capable or competent to assume leadership within the family business, the current leadership can feel most alone, abandoned, and denied the needed support of the family, collectively or individually.

In another view of leadership, the leader can also be mythologized as a messiah or a martyr: a messiah who can secure and preserve the family business against any odds or a martyr who does the same at great personal cost.[11] Unrealistic demands on the leader can be coupled with a sense of over-responsibility, the feeling of being responsible single-handedly for the success of the family business. These two tendencies—messiah or martyr— can lead to isolation from the family and to feeling alone and misunderstood.

Personnel Matters
Related to the deep personal dilemmas of leadership are those of interpersonal relations, the explicit or implicit expectations of—and on—members of the family. Demands or expectations for continuity of the family in leadership positions, on the one hand, and entitlement to positions (keys) on the other, can wreak havoc with the family business. When family or congregational members believe they are entitled to positions, perquisites, or power simply by virtue of their membership in the congregation rather than by competence, training and experience, untold damage can ensue.

Family businesses can be made to settle for less qualified leaders when forced to employ or retain family members, as sometimes happens when there is a requirement that a position of leadership only be filled by a member of the family or congregation. The family workplace then becomes a safe haven for the lesser qualified or competent, thereby potentially eroding the good reputation and potential viability of the family business.

On the other hand, family and congregational members can be made to feel obligated to stay on the job, sometimes long after they are able to make a competent contribution, because of family pressure not to step down or aside. Recent examples of this pressure are Mother Teresa who was asked to remain in her position as superior of the congregation, long after she expressed a desire to be relieved of the responsibility. Likewise, Theodore Hesburgh extended his tenure as president of the University of Notre Dame because a suitable replacement could not immediately be identified among the ranks of the Holy Cross priests, a requirement for the presidency. The pressures the family, as well as others, can place on its leader are immeasurable.

The politics of succession planning, another shadow dimension of leadership, can lead to expectations of entitlement by family members based on seniority or even membership in the family itself. These dynamics can be debilitating in the family. On the one hand, they can rob the person in leadership of the affective and public support needed for the responsibilities assumed for and on behalf of the very family whose behaviors enervate the leader. Or, conversely, they can deprive the family business of the most effective leadership when one is not available from within the family—yet tradition dictates a family member must be appointed.

Overstaying one's usefulness to the business is a particular danger for religious who often tend to be accused of "workaholism" to begin with. How many congregations have jokingly canonized foremothers who literally died on the job? Here, as elsewhere, family dynamics can be particularly threatening to the viability of the business and to non-family members within the organization. When membership in the family is a prerequisite for leadership, the rift created by an atmosphere of "us" and "them" can be corrosive.

Kets de Vries observes that jealousy, envy, and the "spoiled child" syndrome can be found in the convergence of family and business. Family members can consciously or unconsciously triangulate the heads of the family and of the business in order to have their individual needs met. Sibling rivalry, noted above, may be particularly debilitating in dysfunctional family groups, and many religious congregations can point to experiences of sibling rivalry throughout the years. Paradoxically, positions of power and influence can at times be viewed as "rewards" for individual members or as ways of recognizing members for a variety of reasons which do not pertain to the specific competencies of the individual or the position.

Conversely, there can be a "leveling" phenomenon among siblings in a family and in a congregation, an effort to keep all members on the same plane, treating them equally, singling no one out for special attention or recognition, lest one appear to be favored over another. While this identification of behavior characteristic of siblings in a family is not exhaustive, a mere sampling of some of these behaviors underscores their similarity to roles and responses often experienced by members of the congregation within the family business.

Kets de Vries underscores the need for "intraphysic separateness" of family and business, analogous to the human need for individuation. When the family and the business become intertwined as one and the same, the politics and potential dysfunction of the one spill over to the other. When inextricably linked together, the business of the family and the family business can drag each other down and make resolving the unique problems of each almost impossible. This phenomenon mirrors the confusion resulting from the lack of differentiation between the mission of the congregation and mission of its ministries.

Mission and vision, culture, leadership, and personnel matters are four forces at play in all business that have significant ramifications in the family business of religious congregations. Coupled with the shadow sides of each of these forces is the degree of control and involvement exercised by the family and, like the previous four forces, the debate over control and influence can be the source of troublesome conflicts. A summary of the forces at play, positive and negative, appears in Figure 8.

THE CONFLICTS

With the pluses and minuses of mission and values, culture, leadership, and personnel matters established, no discussion of the evolution of family businesses would be complete without a critical examination of the conflicts that arise regarding governance and control. Ownership, or in the context of this discussion, sponsorship, is often equated with control. In most family businesses, control is exercised by the owning family with advice and counsel solicited from professional managers. All major decisions are made by the family itself. Only recently has the notion of influence come into popularity in management circles and sponsorship discussions. Contemporary management literature advocates influence over control. It is popular to speak of alignment and enrollment, empowerment within prescribed parameters.

Figure 8

ADVANTAGES AND DISADVANTAGES
OF FAMILY BUSINESS MODEL

ATTRIBUTE	STRATEGIC ADVANTAGE	POTENTIAL DISADVANTAGE
Vision, Mission	Compelling Sustaining	Divisive: insiders/outsiders Handicapping, viz. RIF
Culture	Source of pride Name: branding Committed stakeholders Reputation and heritage Source of identification	Inflexible Barrier to collaboration Interlocking loyalties Barriers to partnering Clung to irrationally
Leadership	Inherited credibility Charismatic	No-win: "too religious" or "too business-like" Controlling
Personnel Matters	Committed, engaged Early induction into business Continuity Compelled to enter Solidarity	Entitled to positions, power struggles Overstaying usefulness Safe haven Guilty to leave Us/Them

Religious congregations, to the extent that they mirror the attributes of a family business, face the same issues. How much to control; how to direct and yet empower; how to be faithful to the past while at the same time discerning the future. How, and sometimes where, to exercise control and to exercise influence.

Family businesses and sponsoring congregations alike today debate the merits of control versus influence as well as the various points along a continuum between the two extremes. At the inception of many institutional ministries, religious congregations generally held total control of the family business, described earlier as the first wave in the evolution of sponsorship. All governance decisions and a majority of management decisions were made by members of the family; the ministry was viewed as the "Sisters' hospital" or the "Brothers' school."

As described earlier, during the late '60s and early '70s many conditions changed as a result of developments in the Church and in society. In the Church, the Vatican II Council urged all baptized—religious and lay alike—to embrace a greater role in ministries and service within the Church. In society and in the fields of education and healthcare, more opportunities for service were created. As a result, there was a decline in the numbers of women and men entering religious life, thereby creating a shortage of family members for traditional roles in the family business. Additionally, social service ministries in noninstitutional settings often seemed more attractive and appropriate ministerial options to those who were in religious life. Taken together, these forces irrevocably altered the future of the family business.

Moreover, as noted above, this decline in the numbers of family members available for service in the family business occurred at the same time as dramatic increases in the volume, velocity, and complexity of issues facing the ministries occurred. This enabled, on the one hand, more meaningful contributions by qualified laity to traditional family ministries and, on the other hand, greater concern regarding discernment of the appropriate role for members of the religious family. Debates have ensued in chapters and assemblies about whether members of congregations might provide a greater impact or influence in governance and sponsorship roles than in roles in management or in direct service.

Congregations consequently have deliberated about control and influence and how to secure influence over the future direction and integrity of the family business while, at the same time, entering partnership arrangements with other family businesses. These debates and deliberations form the backdrop of the transitions described above. Figure 9 depicts a continuum from control to influence and potential abdication in the case of divestiture. The human dynamics of this continuum deserve some comment.

Kets de Vries points out in the study previously cited that two behaviors can surface at times of transition or diminishment of the family business from total control: enmeshment or entanglement and disengage-ment. Affectively these are normal human responses to loss. In enmeshment, members of the family confuse the appropriate locus of involvement between the family and the business; in other words, they intrude where they should not in business matters, clinging as it were to rights or expectations, to receive information, to be involved in decision making, to be assured of personnel appointments, or the like.

Figure 9

IMPACT RANGE: INFLUENCE-CONTROL

	CONTROL	INFLUENCE and HANDING ON	ENTANGLEMENT	ABANDONMENT
Positions Held by Family	All major positions	Key positions	Select positions	None
Family Affect	Total control	Mutuality	Interference	Disengagement
Impact	Exclusiveness	Shared power	Meddling	Loss
Experience of Others	Working for	Working with	Lack of trust	Replacing

At the other extreme, disengagement from any affective relationship with the family business can be an attempt to shield the family from actually acknowledging and ultimately grieving the transition or loss. This may feel like abandonment to those members of the family still involved in the business. It may also be perceived as inadequate attention to the transition requirements as non-family members assume leadership roles in the business. Both are characteristics of dysfunctional responses to the transition at hand.

Finally, membership in the family business and control of one's destiny are inextricably linked. As the family moves out of direct or total ownership and governance of the ministry and therefore has a lesser role in the shaping of the business, it is easy to see how dysfunctional behavior could develop. Not properly letting go, or letting go without ritualizing or grieving and acknowledging the transition are equally dangerous positions that can create lingering problems for the family business, as well as for members of the family at large. This is further complicated if the family has over-identified with the business. If the handing on can be viewed as a natural step in the evolution of the family business, the response would, of course, be more favorable though not without its experience of loss. The family would then be enabled to see beyond the loss to the "new heirs" or the "next generation."

The lack of new membership, the aging and decline of current membership engaged in the ministry coupled with the need to reposition the family business is a form of death and dying. The central question is how to be faithful and hopeful in the fading. How to see the future as the "harvest of fidelity." How to learn from comparable experiences and case studies from family businesses. How to name and face the reality of transition.

How to embrace and nurture something new and very different from what has been. How to grieve the losses appropriately and how to embrace the new. These are paschal challenges. It is said that true paradigm shifts occur when one does not know what the future will be, only that it will not be as it has been. A spirituality rooted in hope, fidelity, and integrity can assure successful passage through these transitions.

Reflections on Managing Change: Thriving on Chaos

These reflections were originally prepared by one of the authors, Sister Patricia Vandenberg, CSC, as a reflection on change for members of her staff. They have been revised to address the themes of this volume.

Much has been written about the topic of change. Change is part of everyone's life; all of life is constantly changing and renewing itself. Some change is predictable, orderly, planned and executed; some is chaotic. Change and chaos are often linked in our minds and in our lived experiences. Changes often seem to result from or result in chaos. I would like to try to tie these two thoughts together: posing the question of how in the juggernaut of change might we thrive. I am borrowing on two books which I have read and reread: *Change (Paul Watzlawick, et al., 1974)* and *Thriving on Chaos* (Tom Peters, 1991).

These days, rather than deal with change simply at the individual level, we focus on change in a broader context as a complex social phenomenon, in groups, as a corporation, and as a community of committed persons. The experience of being a part of a community of persons, persons committed to a common and compelling mission, can be a significant anchor in the storms of change.

Five dimensions of our human experience impact our response to change: facts, feelings, fate, faith, and fun or fulfillment. Let's reflect briefly on each of these dimensions as we ask ourselves if or how we might remain centered or anchored while in the midst of change which is rapidly accelerating, growing exponentially, and increasing in complexity.

Facts

In talking about change, there are three facts we might all agree on:

- The first is that we are going through massive change right now within our own personal situations, within our ministries specifically, and within society and the Church. Change is more complex and coming at us faster than we have previously experienced.

- The second fact is no surprise: change is disruptive. We do not assimilate change easily into our everyday lives. Even welcomed and positive change is disruptive: our diet is successful but now our clothes don't fit; our promotion comes through but we no longer interact with the same people in the same way; a major transaction or partnership comes to fruition but we are faced with the new challenge of deep cultural integration. All change, the positive as well as the negative, alters our "comfort zone" in some way.

- Third, if we understand what is happening, we can better cope and become more resilient in the face of change. The trick is to learn how to *be* more resilient—individually and collectively. One of the critical factors in successfully navigating the white waters of change is resiliency.

Feelings

We can hear the facts, but we may hear them differently—depending on our feelings. It is important to understand that there are no right and no wrong feelings. I read a book recently about negative emotions called *Shadows of the Heart: A Spirituality of the Negative Emotions* by James and Evelyn Whitehead. In this work, they discuss how some feelings, especially anger, are perceived as negative. Yet anger, paradoxically, can be the single most important positive feeling if it motivates us to action. Think about it: no major social justice change has taken place because people were happy with the current reality. Of course, this does not mean we can give expression to angry feelings in a destructive fashion. Rather, anger can help us get to the heart of the matter. In dealing with change, we must use our feelings—even the negatives ones—for positive action.

Fate

Is it fate that we are going through an upheaval at this time?

In my office, I have a framed episode of the cartoon "Hagar." Hagar is shouting from the top of a mountain to the sky, asking "Why me?" A voice from the heavens answers, "Why not?" We may sometimes feel as Hagar and wonder, why is this change happening to me? Why now? There really are no firm answers to this question, except perhaps the one posed to Hagar. If we ponder our "fate," we can often see that there is more to a situation than appears on the surface. As we move through these changes, we need to continue to learn from our experiences. It is this attribute that marks us as a learning/discerning organization.

Faith

What does our faith tell us? In whom or what do we have faith? Many of us would say we have faith in God. In times of difficulty, we believe that God will not forsake us. Others would say, "I have faith in myself, and no matter what happens, I am confident I have the resources to get through it." Still others have faith in other people, believing that the support network of family, friends, and coworkers will help handle any situation.

Sometimes we put our faith in institutions. What I want to underscore here is that we need to have faith in *the endurance of our mission* and not necessarily in the future of our institutions in their current configurations, including their sponsorship configuration. Institutions endure, but they also have to change themselves many times over to be responsive to current needs.

Fun and Fulfillment

And finally, the aspect of "fun." When I first considered my comments, I titled them "Facts, Feelings, Fate, and Faith." Upon further reflection, I realized that we must be able to find ways to have fun—fulfillment and joy—amidst the numerous changes we experience each day. Despite the difficulties of change, we need to find ways to help each other stay upbeat, energized and positive.

We have our own facts and feelings to deal with each day. We have a unique experience of the fate of living in this time of massive change in so many aspects of our lives, our ministries, our society, and we have a personal set of beliefs and faith that sustains us. I believe we can look together for the learnings that change can bring and find fun and fulfillment, even if it may seem like the proverbial needle in a hay stack.

As we grow in our experience of being a community of committed persons, let us pray that we will have the resilience to not only survive these changes, but maybe to one day say we learned how to thrive on chaos!

PART II

Questions for Personal or Group Reflection

❖

- Where is my organization along the continuum in the shift from the family business?

- What trigger events have we experienced and can we point to which have set in motion this evolution?

- Can we name some facts and accompanying feelings we have recently experienced which will alter the face of our sponsorship?

- Recall experiences or events from the past that signaled the beginning of the end of the "family business" model. What were they? How did they feel?

- What was done proactively to address these feelings of loss or change?

- Are there any lingering feelings about these changes?

PART III

Creative Fidelity

*"I am not scared," she said. "Well, maybe, a little.
Little fireflies of fright light up now and then
when I think about the future."*

Anonymous Sponsor
reflecting on imminent changes
in the sponsorship of her institutional ministry

CREATIVE FIDELITY:
"HOLD ON TIGHTLY, LET GO LIGHTLY"

Traditionally, women and men religious have not been afraid to embrace and welcome both the challenges and risks inherent in the paschal mystery. Today's risk is no less painful; it requires no less courage and faith than yesterday's. Fidelity to a congregation's mission while, at the same time, endeavoring to create something new requires deep faith and lasting hope. All major life changes occasion an experience of loss and must be acknowledged, ritualized, and grieved appropriately. This is true whether the change be perceived to be a positive one, such as a promotion, a successful diet, a relocation, or perceived as negative, such as the loss of a relationship, a job, or a dream. Not matter how the change is perceived, acknowledgment and ritualization of the change/loss are necessary components of a healing transition process.

There are certain predictable experiences in loss. Although they are not linear, moving through the stages is necessary in order to be at peace with the new. Loss, unacknowledged or unattended, can fester until it finds a release or an appropriate avenue of expression or grieving. Grieving tends to be circular; a newer loss can bring back all the experiences of previous losses. The work of grieving is critical and essential to moving on and beyond the direct and immediate experience of loss. There are tools and rituals that can help with this important work. In this section, reminders of the importance of acknowledging and eventually accepting losses are underscored; processes and rituals for memorializing the loss are offered. Additionally, some of the impediments or stumbling blocks to moving on successfully will be noted as well. Not enough emphasis, however, can be placed on the importance of this dimension in the process of moving to sustainable sponsorship for the next millennium.

One very poignant story illustrates the essential need for grief work:

> *It had been over a decade since the sponsoring congregation had sold the hospital to the local town authorities. In an ambulance, now struggling for her last breath, was the former superior during whose administration the transfer had occurred. Stricken by a fatal heart attack, the sister died en route to the hospital.*

> *Back at the motherhouse infirmary, word
> of her death spread like wildfire. On hearing
> the news, one elderly sister who had been
> the medical-surgical supervisor at that
> hospital for 35 years, smiled and observed,
> "Serves her right. She sold the place out
> from under us!"*[12]

How sad, but how real, that several years later unfinished grief work would resurface and in such a manner. The importance of place, the importance of one's role in an organization, the identity of self with the place or the role are all critical elements in the grieving process. Each must be recognized for what it is and dealt with accordingly.

Navigating the white waters of change and transition is difficult for all the individuals involved as well as the sponsoring congregations. An understanding of the predictable stages of grieving, as discussed above, is essential as well as recognizing that to make a new beginning ineluctably requires one to make an ending. Endings are often painful, difficult, and have their own rhythm. William Bridges in his work, *Transitions: Making Sense of Life's Changes,*[13] identifies four necessary components of endings: disengagement, disidentification, disenchantment, and disorientation. Both the original family and the new family will experience these requisite aspects of transitions, although they are considerably less traumatic for the new family.

Viewed from the perspective of the sponsoring congregation, the first aspect, disengagement, requires the
individual and the congregation to release the hold
previously maintained over the ministry. It requires
a pulling back or pulling away, releasing the ministry—
first in partnership and ultimately in a full release—
to others, the new family who will assume responsibility
for the ministry. To some, this can be a painful wrench-
ing, as evidenced by the refrain "it used to be ours...."

To understand the ramifications of disidentification, the
second dimension, one must relate back to the earlier
discussion of the dangers of the overidentification of the
congregation or its individual members with a specific
ministry. This aspect of grief work is also another reason
why it is imperative that the mission of the sponsored
ministry, while rooted and grounded in that of the
congregation, must be viewed as distinct from the
congregation. In other hands, that sponsored ministry
and its mission will go on—so, too, will the mission
of the congregation, albeit in new and different ways
after the transition.

For self-identity to be tied to one's work or ministry
is not unique to religious. When this work is disrupted,
the self-definition of the individual or group may be
threatened as a result. It will be necessary for those
involved to forge new self concepts, new self-identity
differentiated from the specific works.

Disenchantment can be readily identified as a third component. Congregations with long histories and pioneering heritages might be susceptible to believing that the transitions are only temporary and will pass. Today it is most unlikely that, even with a resurgence in the growth of new membership, there will be a return to the 1950s-1960s and to large numbers of members serving in the family business. For one thing, newer ministries seem to be more compelling and, in the minds of some, more congruent with the original or founding vision of the congregation. Challenged with the need to develop new competencies, such as influence in lieu of control, frustrated with the lack of interest of newer members in joining the family business, today's sponsors at times express disenchantment, a natural and expected response to the transitions at hand.

Lastly, current sponsors will experience disorientation or, as Bridges describes it, the "neutral zone." This is the experience of being "between": the present is not the past and the future is unclear. Doubt, fear, concern, anxiety, even guilt—all are components of disorientation. Trying to understand what is happening and why, and where it is all going are natural. Popularly referred to as "paradigm shifts," these experiences are marked by uncertainty and frustration. In a true paradigm shift, the future is unknown, undefined and uncertain.

When these four aspects are viewed from the perspective of the members of the new family, as it were, the reality is no less daunting. Disengagement, disorientation, disidentification, and disenchantment are identifiable responses to the transition. Anecdotes from systems and sponsors who have begun the movement to a juridic person model, for example, reveal real fears and concerns. In particular, board members have asked for clearly defined competencies and accountabilities before assuming the role of sponsor or cosponsor. Some have determined that the responsibility is too great, too nebulous or too demanding, and have declined the privilege of serving in this capacity. Clearly, for an executive or a trustee to assume the role of sponsor requires the integration of a new self-definition and identity.

The expectation that the sisters would always be there, and be there in the role of responsible agent/sponsor, has been shattered. Stepping up to the new responsibility with its risks, demands, personal responsibility and accountability, is awesome and something for which many judge themselves to be unprepared.

Disengaging from a secondary role, "whatever the sisters want," places new and serious responsibilities on the shoulders of the succeeding sponsors—even when this is in the role of cosponsor or partner. As noted earlier, the Church itself lacks experience in dealing with the laity as sponsor. For example, in the fall of 1998 the Vatican called an international conference for "consecrated women" to address the future of the Church's healing mission in the face of the millennium. In the United States, at least, a rapidly diminishing number of Catholic healthcare systems are headed by religious women. The same may be said for many Catholic colleges and universities. Lay partnership is—and has been—a reality in sponsored ministries for many years. The same may be said for many leadership positions in mission and, in some cases, sponsorship in Catholic systems; they are and have been filled with lay men and women.

Hope in a future yet defined, confident in the providence of God as evidenced throughout history, committed to forging intentional, accountable, and supportive communities committed to the same mission and values, those travelling through the white waters of change and transition will discover and create new identities, enchantment, engagement and orientation. Two things are clear: the future will never be what has been and, born out of creative fidelity, the ministries of education, social service, and healthcare will be renewed and revitalized and respond to the needs of a new day and new time.

GRIEF: FIVE STAGES

Literature on grieving identifies five customary stages in the process of dealing with loss:

- Denial of the impending reality;

- Anger once the reality is acknowledged;

- Bartering to prevent or forestall the inevitable;

- Despair or despondency over the events and their inevitable consequences; and

- Acceptance.

These stages have been recognized to correlate with every component of the transitions in a family-held business, whether it be the initial movement away from the "mom and pop" shops or the difficult decision to withdraw and transfer sponsorship. Even when the transaction is a merger with another Catholic organization, feelings of betrayal, selling out, guilt or failure can be experienced.

Certain factors affect the degree of loss; for example, the place or location of the ministry plays an important role. When what was once a place sacred to the family, a place where family members served for years, is no longer in the ownership of the family, particularly when it goes to another use, the sense of loss is intensified. Congregational members are sometimes not even able to drive by former ministry sites that are now parking lots, strip malls or other such sites. In a recent work of fiction, *North of Hope*, the author Jon Hassler poignantly captures a former priest and seminary teacher's reaction when he and his wife return to the site of the seminary, which is now the college where their daughter will be attending. As he enters one of the buildings, a flood of memories returns:

> *He pulled open the heavy, Gothic door that in years past had led him to prayer, and they stepped into the noise of country music and the chatter of four or five dozen students sitting at square little tables. The Church of St. Thomas Aquinas was now the Student Center. They lingered only long enough for Frank to point out that the sanctuary had become a snack bar, the stained glass windows replaced by clear panes, and the choir loft had been remodeled to accommodate pinball machines and video games. "I said a thousand Masses where the fry cook is working," he said. "I preached a hundred sermons on the spot where the Coke machine stands."[14]*

"I said a thousand Masses where the fry cook is working": how poignant the loss, renewed and reawakened upon this visit. Openness in dealing with such feelings, honesty in acknowledging the spectrum of emotions, and facilitation of the process of grieving and letting go will ease the transition and minimize anxiety, hurt, and even hostility. Unless these emotions are dealt with, they will reappear some way or in some form at a later date inappropriately, as with the retired sister who had not dealt with her anger at the sale of the hospital.

In the transition from one wave in the evolution of sponsorship to another, in the loss of the benefits and advantages of the prior relationship, something significant is taken away and missed. The very existence of the franchise mode of sponsorship, as a form of intermediate transition, is, in part, a way to retain the benefits of the earlier state, the experience of control and influence, continuity of leadership, and other important aspects of "sponsoring"—in the broadest sense—a ministry.

Having accomplished the work of letting go, the congregation is then free to create a new future full of new possibilities, to explore the rich potential of sponsorship as partnership, to become excited by the possibility of refounding the ministry with a new family, of reaping the harvest of fidelity. Acknowledging that things will never be the same can free the congregation to forge new relationships and bonds with the new partners.

The Challenge of Sponsorship Transfer

When collaboration is judged not to be feasible, transfer of sponsorship may be the most prophetic and faithful decision. When a congregation prayerfully discerns that it should withdraw from a corporate ministry—for whatever reason: insufficient resources, remoteness from the motherhouse, a change in the direction of its ministry—the effects of such a decision are widespread. The significance and ramifications of ownership or sponsorship transfer, both personally and collectively, cannot be underestimated. Congregational leaders faced with making the difficult decision about continuing sponsorship often experience feelings of guilt or a sense of unfaithfulness to the mission of the congregation and the mission of the facility—as if the act of transferring sponsorship were a form of betrayal of trust or a personal failure. On the contrary, such a decision may represent the fullest exercise of trust and fidelity to the more transcendent mission of the Church.

The gamut of feelings such a decision generates can range from relief to despair, with all ranges of intensity possible. Anger, grief and a sense of loss, however, are the most common feelings. Often repressed (articulation or exhibition of anger traditionally has not been encouraged), such feelings consequently take an indirect toll on the persons affected. Not infrequently, the major superior or leadership team who made the often painful decision also must bear the brunt of misunderstanding and accusation from many fronts—congregation members, the facility's administration and staff, and the civic community. When such a decision must be made by a chapter according to the constitution of the congregation, the result is the same; however, the burden of the responsibility is spread across a broader base.

Many factors contribute to these feelings of loss, grief, and sometimes guilt. The loss of identity is feared, coupled with a concern that the facility may not continue to provide services in the manner it had in the past with the congregation in control. The experience and the expression of these feelings during this transition period are natural and do not necessarily mean that congregational members disagree with or do not understand the necessity or the inevitability of the changes, but rather must give voice to their feelings in order to move on.

It also is not uncommon for members of the congregation to become hostile and angry—common manifestations of loss and grieving. For women and men religious, an assignment to a facility is not just a job or a career, but a ministry. For some, personal identification, value and worth have come from one's ministry, or the self-identify of the individual and the institution have become one and the same. When the visible signs of that ministry are gone—the institution is closed, sold or transferred—personal diminishment can occur.

The act of withdrawing from an institution or transferring sponsorship may have an even greater effect on individuals whose identity has been tied too closely to a specific ministry or institution. This is not uncommon, particularly when a sponsoring congregation has few institutions and individuals are assigned for long periods of time to one place. To date, few studies are available on the grieving process an individual and a congregation must undergo when a sponsored work is no longer part of its ministry.

When the grieving process can be worked through to acceptance, the individuals and the congregation collectively can embrace the decision for what it is: a decision for the greater Church (transfer of sponsorship) or for the greater good of the civic community (closure, merger with another facility). Deep trust—in the individuals making this decision, in the Spirit who abides in the Church, in the integrity and goodwill of those involved—in addition to careful communication and the involvement of those affected also helps to offset the intensity of the feelings of loss. The paschal mystery teaches that there is no resurrection without the crucifixion, no rebirth without first experiencing death.

RITUALIZATION

Ritualization of the change can enhance and focus the necessary grief work. Recognition of past contributions, celebrations and story telling, remembering and honoring the past are important steps in dealing with the loss and promoting healing. This is a work of stewardship of intangible assets, including the legacy, tradition, and heritage of the congregation in general or at a particular site.

There is a growing body of rituals for specific aspects of the transition. For example, a name change, referred to above, can be ritualized through scriptural story telling: Abram, Saul, Peter, Sarah. Transfer to a new sponsor can be symbolized in seed and planting images. Figure 10 lists other appropriate symbols and their potential use in ritualizing a change, whether it be transfer, divestiture or closure.

Figure 10

SYMBOLS AND RITUALS FOR THE PASSAGES

SYMBOL	THEME/MEANING or USE
Seeds, planting, harvest theme	A time to sow, a time to reap; One sows, another reaps
Timepiece, watch	There is a time for every purpose under heaven
Writing instrument, pen	Opportunity to write a new chapter in our history
Embers	Ignite a new fire; Phoenix

Because individuals grieve differently, congregations will need to manage both individual needs to mourn as well as the corporate or collective need to deal with the changes. As a psychologist specializing in grieving, Dr. Alla Bozarth-Campbell notes that something precious may be created in the activity of grieving by recognizing and expressing the meaning of the loss individuals can share in their common history and ideals. She points out that it is in the act of saying "good-bye" that one can come to an acknowledgment of what prior relationships have meant and give thanks for the past.[15]

Navigating the Loss Incurred by Changes

True empowerment is necessary as each person learns new roles and leaves historical roles behind. At one time or another in the changing of the models of the family business, both the sponsoring group and the new partners will predictably experience a sense of loss and powerlessness. During times such as these, sponsors particularly have expressed feelings of loss of control and of things having gotten out of hand. For the sponsor, there is a shift in priorities for action; for the individual members of the sponsoring congregation, there is a perceived loss of status and privilege in the sponsored works; for the new partner, there are new expectations for contributing to and being accountable for the ministry.

In the "mom and pop" shop model, the family was actively involved in the day-to-day management of the

operations. In the newer models of franchise or partnership, the roles, involvement, and focus of the family must
be placed elsewhere, such as on establishing and maintaining a direction; on succession or continuity
of leadership planning; on leadership development.

In his book, *Organizational Culture and Leadership,* Edgar
Schein identified key differences between founders and
owners and what he called the "professional managers,"
that is, those leaders who succeed family members as
managers within the organization in either the franchise
or the partnership models. He particularly noted that the
orientation of the organization with family members as
managers is local in nature with the local leader needing
high visibility, support, and backing from members of the
family. In the transition from this model, the orientation
of the organization becomes significantly broader; leadership may be invisible and not receive much attention
and cannot rely principally on the support of the family
in promotion of a vision and a culture.

In the later models, the area most affected is the
continuing role of the family in the family business.
As the family becomes less active in management,
it is essential that the family identify and recruit capable
individuals who are committed to keeping the mission
and the ministry alive. This requires careful articulation
of the behaviors, expectations, and competency norms
for leadership. The new leadership, as well as the original

owners, have the task of leading the organization throughout the transition and successful grieving.

Grieving done well and completely can be healing. Old wounds are allowed to close; scars may remain tender, but the wound has healed. New beginnings can, ultimately, be a source of hope and joy as T. S. Eliot writes in "Four Quartets": "To make an end is to make a beginning...." Faith sees the paschal mystery everywhere manifest: from death, to resurrection.

Reflections: The Shattered Mirror

Reflection prepared by Sister Patricia Vandenberg, CSC.

Symbols are critical in human life: they convey meaning and memory, carry the past, point to the future. They often evoke laughter and tears, irony and hope. The memories and the meaning they carry can erupt in the most unexpected circumstances. When they remind us of loss, they are painful; when they lead to the future, they are carriers of promise and joy. In either case, they have tremendous emotional import.

When I was twelve, my father died. He had been ill for some time, and my mother struggled to hold the family together as best she could. Our family had been living in Brooklyn and vacationing over summers on Long Island. This particular summer, as our vacation drew to a close, my father became acutely ill. My sister and I were sent to Kansas City to be with my mother's family. Within a month, he died. In fact, my father died, was buried, and my mother moved us into a new apartment in the city and enrolled us in a new school—before my sister and I came home six weeks later. It was a disorienting experience to have so many things change at once.

At Christmas that year, my sister and I tried to decorate the apartment to create a holiday spirit. We were grieving the loss of my father in so many ways. One day after school while my mother was at work, we decided to decorate the apartment by hanging all the Christmas cards. We taped Christmas cards all around the apartment, including the dresser mirror in my mother's room. Without realizing how unstable the mirror was, we taped cards to it. The mirror crashed to the floor and broke into what seemed like a million pieces.

When my mother came home from work that evening, my sister and I confessed to breaking the mirror. My mother's first response was "Are you girls hurt? Are you all right?" When we indicated that the only damage was to the mirror, she seemed relieved. We both cried, sensing what a loss she must have felt; she remained calm. Later that night as I fell asleep, I heard my mother crying. The dresser and the mirror were gifts from my father and among the only things she brought from our family home to our apartment in the city—and now the mirror was shattered.

What is the meaning of this story? Very simple. There are two lessons to be gleaned: one is the meaning of symbols and the second is the need to complete grief work. Mirrors, logos, icons—all are symbols and carry heavy emotional connotations. For my mother, the mirror was a symbol, a reminder of my father. Its loss was irreparable; it was irreplaceable. Certainly, there were other mirrors, but there would never be another given by my father.

Then there was the grief work. Needing to bury my father, close the vacation house, move to the city, bring my sister and me back to New York, enroll us in a new school— all meant the requisite grieving time was short, distracted by necessary tasks, and unfinished—for her as well as for my sister and me.

My father died nearly forty years ago. My mother is now in her 70s, living in a retirement community in Colorado. She has not had the mirror to hold her memories of my father's love for her and their children. Not a day goes by but that she doesn't miss my father. Our sense of loss lessened over the years, but it is loss nonetheless. Often she will observe an attribute in one of her grand-children that reminds her of my father. His love is mirrored in the next generation.

That Christmas, the shattered mirror was the catalyst for her unfinished grieving—and my sister's and mine as well. Wrapped up in the shattered mirror were all the losses—my Dad, home, familiar neighborhood, parish, and school . . . no longer a family of four.

This little story is a good learning for all of us as we face the passage of the old, familiar, and comfortable ways of doing things. The work of grieving is difficult but inescapable. Without completing this work, the future is encumbered and its potential leashed.

When the family business passes to new hands, however welcomed, there is a loss we may feel. The mirror, the reminder of what has been, is shattered and nothing can take its place. However, life does go on. New life in the form of the next generation brings new joys and hopes and dreams.

My own religious community was forced to sell its oldest hospitals several years back. Whenever I visit that city, a heartache returns. I am past thinking: "Maybe if we had done this, then . . ." "What if . . ." But the pain of loss is still keen. We ritualized the transaction as best we could.

We gathered many of our former employees, trustees, physicians, and our friends to celebrate all the good we had accomplished and to ritualize the transfer to new owners. Over time the pain has lessened.

Our ministry continues in that community, albeit in new forms and new relationships. There is a memorial fountain, but more importantly, the memorial lives on in the hearts of those who carry on the mission today. What was, like the shattered mirror, will never be again. We must accept that.

Our search must be for ways to acknowledge, accept, grieve, and begin anew. We also must honor the past and our many symbols and memories and learn from each of our experiences. I never tape Christmas cards to mirrors.

PART III

Questions for Personal
or
Group Reflection

- How well have I/we dealt with loss and grief in life thus far?

- Where are we experiencing loss currently? How can we encourage and ritualize expressions of loss and grief?

- How good am I/are we at ritualizing the important events in our lives? Do we routinely ritualize important events in the life of our organizations?

PART IV

The Future of Sponsorship

I don't think we have ever given
enough credit to the Sisters
for the growth of the Church in the United States
over a period of a hundred years,
through their schools and hospitals, etc.
Of course, it was an extraordinary working of God's grace.
I guess we'll just have to keep praying
that God will build them up again,
after this slump....

Letter from a former high school chaplain
to the Sisters of Mercy Regional Community of Chicago
December 1997

The Future of Sponsorship

The last decades of the twentieth century will have seen more profound and radical changes in Catholic institutional ministries than at any other time in their history. Two particularly volatile areas—changes in the demographics (fewer and older members) and ministerial focus (away from institutional services) of religious congregations who have historically served as sponsors and the changing requirements of sponsorship itself—have significant bearing on the evolution and, consequently, because of their interrelatedness, on the future of ministry. Using the family business metaphor developed and elaborated on earlier in this volume, this section will focus on approaches to the future: defining the competencies required for the next generation of sponsors.

The Shift

In order to be positioned for the future, for a future which is viable and strong, today's sponsoring congregations need to articulate their future locus of and requirements for sponsorship. They will need to identify the competencies which will be required of sponsors—religious and lay—in the future, and to implement plans to identify and develop sponsors with these competencies. Failure to address these critical areas in a timely and focused way could inevitably lead to the diminishment or, worse, to the loss of the ministry in the future. In order to examine more fully the challenges to fidelity and sponsorship, this section will first summarize the forces at play in the environment, then identify the changes in congregational focus before discussing the how and what of sponsorship in the future.

Today, perhaps as never before in their history, Catholic institutional ministries have a critical and vital role to play in American culture and society. These institutions can help to sustain a culture of compassionate and excellent service which fosters respect for the persons who are served. They can also help to raise a voice of ethical consciousness, moral reflection, and passionate insistence on the continuing transformation of American society. The issues raised by the changes cited earlier in this volume have at times seemed daunting to current sponsors and have caused some congregational and diocesan sponsors to question whether they can remain in institutional ministry at all or if, in the interest of the greater good, they should transfer sponsorship of their ministries. And if they choose to remain, the subsequent question arises: whether congregational sponsors maintain the role of sponsor or serve as hands-on providers of services?

Believing that without a firm institutional or organizational presence one cannot have an effective moral voice, this section is premised on continuing institutional ministries, thereby continuing the transformation of American society. The Church and society would be poorer without the presence or with a diminished presence of Catholic institutional ministries, providers and sponsors. What is needed without doubt is a clearly articulated vision for Catholic institutional ministries in the face of today's massive changes and a well-defined plan of action to secure their future presence and participation in American society.

Religious congregations which have historically served in the role of sponsors for most institutional ministries in the United States have been undergoing profound changes in recent decades, particularly since the Vatican II Council. Four forces impact the future of sponsorship and have a profound impact on the founding religious congregations or families: their changing demographics; a strong bias among some members to serve in noninstitutional ministry settings; the sometimes strained ecclesial relations over ethical issues and institutional self-governance; and the velocity and complexity of technical issues facing institutional ministries themselves.

The previous discussion concerning the evolution of sponsorship will set the context for examining the transition to the next generation. Since the formal institutionalization of sponsorship about three decades ago, three evolutionary waves have been identified: the first has been described in terms of a family business; the second, continuing the business analogy, as a franchise; and the present wave as a partnership or alliance. Figure 11 summarizes the major operational characteristics at play in these three waves.

As may be gleaned from the above, significant cultural changes are necessarily induced in the process of evolution. Communication, control, accountability, even the very articulation or translation of the mission of the organization are affected by the gradual evolution to new modes of sponsorship. In the eyes of some beholders, these changes are eclipsed by the changes occurring within the family of the sponsoring congregation.

American religious congregations have fewer members to continue either the family business, the ministry of direct service, or the ministry of sponsorship and governance of established ministries. In other words, the founding families no longer have the numbers of family members with interest or, in some cases, energy to maintain the family business. So much has already been written about both the aging of congregational members and the decline in the numbers of members

Figure 11

HISTORICAL CHARACTERISTICS:
THREE OF THE WAVES OF SPONSORSHIP

	FIRST WAVE	SECOND WAVE	THIRD WAVE
Operative model	Family-run operation	Franchise	Partnership
Locus of family influence	Presence and numbers	Governance, management	Governance
Prevailing posture of family	Can seem distant and removed	Less distant	Open; sharing
Pattern of communications	Restricted to family principally	More open; often two-way	Two-way
Model of relating	Family independent of other partners	Family still independent; others consulted on occasion	Interdependent
Climate or atmosphere	Rigid and rule bound	Growing openness	Trusting, open
Accountability framework	Top-down	Top-down with some input from others	Mutually (family and partners) agreed upon
Source of control	Rules and dominance of family members	Prescribed standards of accountability	Mutual accountabilities
Origin of vision and mission statements	Family members, often only head of family	Initiated by family, others with limited input	Shared process of theological reflection and dialogue
Principal time perspective	Present	Past-present; preservation of past	Present-future
Family role	Staff, management, governance	Principally governance and management	Principally governance

available for governance-sponsorship service that the reality need not be repeated here.

These factors, coupled with the continued growth in members' interest in and desire to serve in noninstitutional or seemingly more justice oriented ministries, have impacted the numbers of sisters available for service in governance or sponsorship.[16] Moreover, the role of those family members within institutional ministries has changed and will continue to change dramatically. These changes require different skills within and without the family from those required when the family was active in operations and management. (See Figure 12.)

When these internal changes are juxtaposed against changing and challenging external environmental forces, it is not surprising to find traditional congregational sponsors exploring new models for sponsorship and/or examining the desirability of moving to some form of public or private juridic model, wherein the requirements of congregational sponsorship are fulfilled by a board or other specifically designated groups of persons. The movement toward the public or private juridic person may occur within the third wave, that is in the formation of a partnership with the laity in a new juridic person. For some sponsors, the creation of a new juridic person and the withdrawal of the family is, in reality, a fourth wave.

Figure 12
FAMILY BUSINESS IN TRANSITION

FROM	TO
Active management	Succession planning with leadership formation and development
Operations	Governance
Mission and philosophy development	Mission integration and accountability

There are certain distinctions that can be noted between a public and a private juridic person. A public juridic person is the "corporate person," publicly recognized as responsible for those assets identified as stable patrimony or ecclesiastical goods, governed by the requirements of Canon Law, and used in the service of the Church. In the past, the public juridic person responsible for institutional ministries has generally been the congregation or diocese which founded or currently owns the assets of the ministry.[17] The private juridic person, as distinguished from the public juridic person, is held responsible primarily for the conduct of the operations of the ministry, and the property is not ecclesiastical goods. Regardless into which direction the family moves in the future, certain steps are critical to the transition.

It should be underscored that what is actually being sponsored today has changed from the sponsorship of institutional ministries in established buildings and facilities to the sponsorship of schools without walls, satellite campuses, institutions with distance learning; integrated health delivery structures, partnerships, and networks in a variety of complex and interdependent relationships. Not meaning to minimize the responsibilities of sponsorship when services were contained within institutional structures, one must nevertheless argue that sponsorship of newer, more innovative modes of service delivery, whether in education or healthcare, poses newer and unfamiliar questions and risks.

In the wake of these changes, a corresponding shift in the issues faced by current sponsors also occurs. No longer is sponsorship primarily focused on the buying, selling, mortgaging, or otherwise encumbering of Church property. Sponsors are called to approve partnerships, joint ventures, outreach initiatives, and other interwoven patterns of networking which blur the identity of Church ownership. Sponsors are expected to do so with an eye to the ability of the newly formed organization to be faithful to the mission and values inherent in the ministry; to be creative in responding to emerging needs; and to be discerning in moving into new relationships. In the final analysis, because the very focus of sponsorship will have changed, sponsors of the future will need a new set of skills beyond those required in the past.

Many of the congregational sponsors of institutional ministries have begun to explore the desirability or feasibility of moving toward the option of public or private juridic persons. These developments are cause for reflection. What does it mean to sponsor today? What actually is sponsored, as institutional ministries change in response to environmental forces and settings? What will be the focus of the sponsorship agenda in the future? What attributes or competencies must the next generation of sponsors, lay or religious, possess? These are the critical questions facing us today—the answers to which will indelibly reshape the face of American Catholic institutional ministries.

The Starting Point

To create a future for institutional ministries as strong and vital as their past will require serious discernment regarding sponsorship. Framing the questions and leading the stakeholders through this process is a complex undertaking. (See Figure 13.) What is often lacking is a well developed and articulated theology of sponsorship as a foundation on which to build models or articulate and evaluate alternatives. Over the years, not all sponsors have carefully or systematically addressed the need for this theological foundation. Today, the need cannot be ignored. Institutional ministries must be rooted in an articulated theology for sponsorship, one which is grounded in a Gospel spirituality and in post-Vatican II ecclesiology. These footings are essential to the further evolution and maturation of the ministry—without which there will be only a non-intentional (and perhaps unintended) future.

Figure 13

CRITICAL QUESTIONS FOR DISCERNMENT

- What does it mean to sponsor today? What is actually "sponsored?"

- Where will the focus of sponsorship be in the future?

- What skills must sponsors possess in this new environment?

THREE STEPS IN THE TRANSITION PROCESS

Three steps are necessary for the success of the evolution to whatever model of cosponsorship and/or juridic person is selected: permission, preparation, and praxis.[18] The first fundamental step is permission: recognizing, ritual-izing, and accepting the fact of change. The permission stage requires the members of the sponsoring religious congregation individually and collectively to recognize and accept the fact that the paradigm has shifted away from the familiar, comfortable, family-controlled model of the past. This may not occur without a deep sense of loss for what has been. With this permission, as it were, to accept the evolution of sponsorship and the emergence of new leadership for the family business, the next step is preparation.

Preparation involves the conscious and intentional identification and formation of the next generation of sponsors. In part, this task can be initiated by identifying the competencies necessary to ensure sustainable sponsorship in the future. Preparation requires the founding family to embrace new roles and to learn new skills: skills in succession planning; influence without control, in management of the process of change. Those moving into new roles in the family business must be able to adapt to ambiguity and be willing to accept responsibility for the very integrity of and fidelity to the ministry. Preparation will necessitate a systematic approach to the formation and development of sponsors, building on the excellent work most sponsoring congregations have already begun to form new executive and managerial leadership. Although the new reality will be different, it will be a continuation and an enhancement of the mission and ministry of the founding family, nurtured by years of direct service, growth in spirituality, and a commitment to be faithful to the mission in the face of various internal and external challenges.

The final step in this process is praxis, the union of action and reflection: the rigorous effort to be faithful, to create a new community of persons committed to a common vision, mission and accountability. Prayerful reflection on the demands of the ministry, the signs of the times vis-a-vis the Gospel, and a disciplined approach to discernment are the essential elements. With the new sponsors' focus on creative fidelity, management's emphasis on workplace spirituality and accountability for mission integration, the family business can be assured of a sustainable sponsorship.

Factors that may inhibit the successful transition are manifold. Figure 14 highlights these factors. There may be a historic lack of trust between the old and new sponsors; insufficient preparation of the next generation; lack of experience in such critical ingredients as sharing power, integrating an apostolic spirituality, and utilizing influence where control is not appropriate.

The lack of an articulated theology of sponsorship may cripple the effort to move smoothly to a new stage. In addition to this, there is the Church's inexperience to relate to lay leadership. On the other hand, to facilitate successful transition, an articulated theology of sponsorship can be an anchor through the change process.

Figure 14

POTENTIAL IMPEDIMENTS TO SMOOTH TRANSITION

AREAS OF CAUTION
• Lack of trust in each other (old and new sponsors)
• Lack of trust in the Church itself
• Insufficient preparation on either side (old sponsors to accept change; new sponsors to be ready for new role)
• Reluctance to "step to the plate" on the part of new sponsors

• Lack of experience in
    Sharing power
    Exercising influence rather than control
    Integrating apostolic or public spirituality
    Utilizing discernment in decision making

• Unattended need to acknowledge and accept change and its necessary losses
• Failure to articulate a sound theology of sponsorship
• Official Church's inexperience (or inability) to relate to lay leadership in critical Church ministries

A Theology of Sponsorship

Implicit in the above discussion of change and its attendant consequences is the imperative for an articulated theology of sponsorship. A theology of sponsorship will need to address the challenges to, the direction of, and the radical shaping of its response to the times. This theology must be created in the spirit of praxis. It must acknowledge the call of each person to holiness, to live in a discerning manner, and to self-lessly respond to the legitimate needs of others and the need to do so within the community called Church (*Lumen Gentium, Gaudium et Spes*). It must also situate institutional ministries as vital ministries of the Church.

Such a theology must necessarily be built on both a theology of stewardship and a theology of baptism which calls all to ministry. Stewardship principles stress that what is sponsored has been held in sacred trust. It is not owned—not by the founding congregation nor by the new sponsors. The privilege of serving as sponsor, as steward, is one of service in the reign of God to the poor, the needy, the uneducated, the ill. This theology must also be rooted in an ecclesiology in which the community of committed persons is bound together by a Gospel spirituality, a deep sense of personal and mutual accountability, a commitment to the continuity of the ministry and to fidelity to the mission. This ecclesiology will be rich with hope and promise and attend to the unfolding agenda of Vatican II in calling the people of God to integrity, fidelity, accountability, and generosity in service, in mercy, in justice.

A theology of baptism emphasized in the Vatican II underscores the right and responsibility of each person for the apostolic mission of the Church by virtue of baptism. This right and responsibility cannot be given nor taken away by the Church; it is an element inherent in the sacrament of baptism. While the proper role of the laity in the mission of the Church is a matter of continual discernment and evolution, informed through praxis which is lived reality prayerfully reflected on, it is nevertheless an ineluctable call and responsibility. An area in particular need of a discerning reflection today is the increasing participation by persons of other faith traditions and practices in the executive leadership and governance.

Once a theological foundation has been articulated and reflected upon, praxis must continue and ultimately shift its focus to those individuals who have responsibility for insuring organizational integrity, fidelity to the organizational mission, and the qualities or competencies which sustain and strengthen the ministry. A deep personal spirituality is required. Such a spirituality may best be described as an apostolic spirituality, a commitment to service, to public witnessing of mission and core values, to the pursuit of justice.

THE CONCEPT OF COMPETENCIES

The concept of personal/professional competencies is borrowed from business and refers to those critical skills, behaviors, and attitudes which an individual characteristically and consistently exhibits in performing a certain role or function.[19] In other words, they are "second nature" to the individual—not just those characteristics which are in evidence in a crisis. To apply this notion of core competencies to requirements of sponsorship is a critical first step in preparing the next generation of sponsors.

For the purposes of this discussion, competencies may be clustered into three categories: strategic, cultural, and personal. (See Figure 15.) The strategic qualifications of sponsors at a minimum would include: skill in ethical discernment; social vision embracing social justice, advocacy, and systemic transformation; and requisite business expertise, such as administration or management, health services, finance, insurance, law, etc. Somewhat harder to name and measure are the cultural sensitivities a sponsor will need. These competencies must include an understanding of and sensitivity to the history, tradition, and culture of the organization and its sponsors as well as the capacity to translate historical values into present situations in a complex, dynamic environment. Personal attributes would include a spirituality; the ability to manage conflict and negotiate win-win outcomes; and a capacity for system thinking.

What is needed for today and for tomorrow are sponsors with specific new competencies who remain grounded in fidelity to the heritage of the founding congregation and the mission of the organizations; are committed to assuring the integrity of those organizations as they change in response to market forces and new needs; and understand and promote discernment in all decision making. Finally, the very structure of sponsorship will inevitably be altered in the creation of these networks and partnerships. An organizational structure with the leadership of the congregation as corporate member with reserved powers, in most instances, will not be adaptable to these new structures. The locus of sponsorship itself will most likely shift to the governing board of these organizations. Sponsorship in the future will likely be mediated through governance.

Figure 15

CRITICAL COMPETENCIES FOR FUTURE SPONSORS

AREA	SAMPLE COMPETENCIES

Strategic	• Skill in discernment in decision making
	• Mature social vision
	  (including social justice, advocacy, systemic transformation)
	• Appropriate business expertise
	  (management, law, finance, insurance, etc.)
	• Comfort with risk taking

Cultural	• Sensitivity to culture, history and tradition of sponsors • Ability to translate historical values to current situations • Passionate concern for the poor • Capacity for ambiguity
Personal	• Personal (public or apostolic) spirituality or centeredness • Ability to manage conflict; commitment to achieve win-win • Capacity for system thinking • Appropriate self-reliance

In many of these new arrangements, sponsorship will be limited to parts of the organization which have a public identity as Catholic. The sponsor will often not be the sponsor of the entire entity, but only of some of its elements. The sponsor will not always be, and more likely most commonly will not be, the majority or controlling partner; and the sponsor may own what will not always be the most central or critical components. These shifts, while seemingly subtle, will have a profound effect on the manner in which sponsorship is exercised as well as the qualities required in the sponsors.

THE NEXT GENERATION

Personal characteristics of the next generation of sponsors must include the ability to negotiate win-win resolutions; to place common good and Catholic/Christian identity before the historical self-identity of the organization while remaining firmly rooted in the original founders' vision; and to be able to say no when ethical discernment directs nonparticipation. These are relatively new skills for sponsors who historically may have operated under a different set of norms and ground rules more appropriate to a family-owned business than a highly complex economic partnership.[20]

Foundational to assuring sponsorship in the next generation is belief in the power of the organizational values to influence, and the spirit and spirituality of the sponsor to animate the transformation of American institutional ministries—an influence that is posited on Catholic institutional ministries remaining active players. Moreover, a spirit of courage and daring, rooted in personal and organizational integrity, is essential. Together with a spirit of detachment from individual corporate or congregational identity and a willingness to forge those partnerships, sponsors can insure the future viability of sponsored ministries.

Foremost among the accountabilities of the sponsors in the next generation are: the creation of communities of persons committed to a shared vision and common core values to create, as it were (continuing the metaphor of a family business), an "extended family" with significant responsibility in the business. Additionally, the willingness to engage in rigorous ethical discernment about resource allocation, selection of partners, and service and strategic opportunities is essential, as is the successful translation and transporting of values into new partnerships and new organizational structures without relying on those vehicles which have made us successful in the past. It goes without saying that the next generation of sponsors must have a deeply integrated spirituality and a passionate concern for the poor and disenfranchised.

Power: Control or Influence
This reflection would not be complete without expanding on the debate in Catholic institutional ministries today on the question of control versus influence. Historically, congregations owned, operated and governed facilities—

they thereby had control over these assets. This is certainly not the case today. With the growth of collaborative initiatives and partnerships, today's sponsors must of necessity sponsor in a mode of influence. And to influence requires radically different skills from those required to control—skills most sponsors do not feel they possess at this time.

The Creation of New Communities

The final feature of these emergent new models is an intentional community of persons who share the same commitment to mission and ministry and to creative fidelity.[21] Interdependence and mutuality, co-responsibility and reciprocal accountability are critical components in the formation of this community. There is a vulnerability and a fragility to something new. It needs to be nurtured and tended. A compassionate spirit of collaboration must characterize each person's participation and must prevail between the two generations of sponsors in the actual transition. There is a sense of letting go as well as taking hold. The congregation must, in the words of a John Denver song, "hold on tightly, let go lightly" while the new generation of sponsors takes hold and moves into the future.

The new community must be able to forge a new identity from the legacy of the family business, suitable and adaptable for the future. A certain cohesiveness comes from pioneering something new. Families have their own cohesiveness; no relationship endures longer than that of the family. In this paradigm shift, a new community must be formed with "outsiders," a community strong enough to carry the family business into the future. This is what is meant by sustainable sponsorship—after the founding family's participation and control have passed. As the strong hold of control is loosened in the movement away from the family business to the new family, as it were, fidelity manifests itself in a commitment to a common vision and mission and to accountability for the same.

In summary, then, today's sponsors must find the energy to develop the next generation of sponsors which may be made up of members of the congregation in whom these competencies have been developed; or in joint partnerships with laity sharing in the role of sponsor, or of laity alone who have been prepared to serve as sponsor. How do we begin to prepare the next generation to be faithful stewards of the ministry and thus secure a Catholic presence in American education and healthcare? As these changes continue and the velocity and volume of change accelerates, the questions which must be asked are: What will sponsorship mean? What must this generation of sponsors impart to the next generation?

In this transition from a family business to a franchise or a partnership, the roles of each player have changed—

sometimes subtly and sometimes dramatically. Because the roles of the sponsor and those of the partner have and will continue to evolve, two activities are necessary during the critical period: the empowerment of sponsor and partner and the acknowledgment of the losses accompanying these changes. Without both activities, smooth transition is not possible. The most cherished promise in these times of change is that found in Jeremiah: "See I do a new thing among you. . . [and] plans to give you a future full of hope" (Jeremiah 29:11).

Reflections:
Tell the Next Generation

This reflection by Sister Patricia Vandenberg, CSC, was originally presented at a Consolidated Catholic Health Care Governance Forum in February 1996. It has been revised for this book.

Let me start my reflection by explaining the origin of the title: Tell the Next Generation. At the beginning of Advent this past year, I picked up a book that I had not read since 1981 titled *Tell the Next Generation: Homilies and Near Homilies*. The author and eminent Jesuit theologian, Walter J. Burghardt, was a frequent homilist at the Dahlgren Chapel of Georgetown University where I frequently worshiped when I lived in Washington, D.C.

Things seemed so much simpler in the '70s when he wrote many of these homilies. As I scanned the index, I noticed a homily titled "Don't Be Afraid: Advent for the Medical Profession." As I read the simple, four-page homily, I was deeply moved and asked myself why. What Burghardt says of physical illness is also true of our spiritual experience these days. He wrote that as you encounter hospitalized patients, you see fear in their eyes. You realize they are afraid because it may hurt. They are afraid because they feel alone. They are afraid because they may die.

That was exactly how I was feeling as I struggled with the question of sponsorship: it was hurting. I did feel alone, and, yes, the institution of sponsorship as I had known it was already dying. And I do not know what to tell the next generation of Catholic healthcare executives, trustees and sponsors—except to tell them the truth: I am searching for the meaning of sponsorship in this moment and for the future.

As I finished reading the homily, I realized just how deeply I was struck by the question itself: What would I tell my sisters about the evolution of this ministry over the next generation, about these past twenty-five years and into the next century? What am I trying to tell the next generation of sponsors about the evolving meaning of sponsorship in the United States during these closing years of the twentieth century? What will sponsorship look like in the next millennium?

There is a great deal of discussion these days about models of sponsorship. There has been candid admission of the challenges and difficulties in moving the sponsorship question to the fore, as well as sharing of the successes and accomplishments of new or transitional models. If we think of sponsorship in terms of architecture, what we see currently is the structure above ground. What I think we need to do more, however, is to examine the foundation and the underpinnings of sponsorship, namely, our ecclesiology.

When most of us were growing up, when someone said "church," we immediately thought of a building that was the parish church. We might even offer a commentary on the pastor or parish priests and sisters. But by the mid-1960s, when someone said "church," many of us would think of the people of God in light of Vatican II. Our whole notion of Church had shifted dramatically from bricks and mortar to a living body. If we were very attuned to Vatican II, we might even have puzzled over the role of the Church in the modern world. A whole new notion of ecclesiology was emerging. Never again would we equate Church with a building.

There were debates at chapters about sponsorship and the meaning—and value—of institutional ministries. Some congregations wrestled with these questions and answered by moving out of institutional sponsorship altogether. In others, the debate continued, sometimes creating camps among the members, those who worked in corporate structures which were seen as "big businesses" and those who did more direct service which was perceived as "real ministry with the poor."

In my own congregation, the Sisters of the Holy Cross, we struggled at one chapter with a preposition: Would we say "ministry *to* the laity" or "ministry *with* the laity?" A critical distinction and one which revolved around our very ecclesiology. When the vote was taken, ministry with the laity was our stance. Coming out of that chapter in 1984, I thought we enjoyed the wind of the Spirit at our back moving us along in our evolving notion of sponsorship.

In 1992 when we embarked on a major sponsorship reflection process, we had the benefit of eight years of intentional movement in our ecclesiology. What were we telling ourselves about sponsorship—let alone, what would we tell the next generation? Since structure follows strategy, we needed to have a clear strategy or theology of sponsorship before we could address the structural nature of sponsorship.

Articulating a theology is no small task in a congregation of increasingly diverse theological perspectives. A critical moment in the pursuit of this theological un-derpinning came when the president of the congregation addressed the leadership of the health system, saying, "You are the leaders of a *community of committed persons* we call the Holy Cross Health System." A *community of committed persons*—the expression filled the air that day and has echoed in our hearts and minds throughout the intervening years. Building on the insights of Juan Luis Segundo, SJ, in his landmark book, *The Community Called Church,* the president had in fact announced a shift in our ecclesiology as we came to see and to name ourselves as Church, as a community of persons committed to a common mission and values. Her notion of Church was inclusive and anchored in the present reality of our ministry in partnership with the laity. Her lens was the Gospel and her eyes were always searching out the poor and marginalized. She would not allow us to retreat in the face of conflict in the marketplace, but rather compelled us to enter more deeply into the fray, seeking a just and compassionate resolution to even the most thorny challenges we face. Segundo's belief is that the community called Church possesses the secret of what is happening in human history, knows its warp and woof, and understands the stakes that are playing out. He goes on to write about faith, love, self-giving, mystery, deep roots, and firm foundations. His litany describes so well the characteristics of our ministry today.

What insights might we draw from this story of the evolution of one congregation's theology and ecclesiology of sponsorship? There are five lessons I would like to draw out:

- There is no meaningful movement without first clarifying your *vision*—your vision of Church and of ministry.

- It is not sufficient for religious to clarify the vision and tell the laity. We must *live into the vision together*, engaging in an active dialogue, acknowledging that some of our questions do not have answers in the present moment, but that we will be graced as we live into those answers.

- Typically, there is a *trigger event* or events which set the process of evolution in motion.

- There is no substitute for *sound theological reflection* in this process. Sponsorship is built on the foundation of a theological base. It is not a matter of personal charism or congregational heritage alone and least of all external structures.

- It takes time to *shift the paradigm of sponsorship*, but the shift can only happen if the leadership announces it, encourages it to occur, and affirms its evolution and mentors the new sponsors.

Allow me now to return to Father Burghardt's homily. Why was I moved so deeply by the theme, "Don't be afraid"? When we set out to change our vision of sponsorship, we are often beset by fears. We fall prey to:

- Fears that letting go of the old model may hurt. This is especially true if sponsorship of institutions is critical to the self-identity of the congregation itself.

- Fears that we may feel alone if we exercise prophetic leadership within our congregation and other members are not ready.

- Fears that something in us may die. We believe that death leads to resurrection and yet it is often a fearful human experience.

- Fears that the laity may not be ready to accept additional responsibility for this ministry.

- Fears that lay leaders will assume responsibility but become distracted by the demands of the marketplace. Things that we have cherished for over a century could get lost in the shuffle as business considerations seem to overtake ministry reflection.

- Fears that maybe in the final analysis we should not try to sponsor Catholic educational or healthcare institutions any more and that we are not really listening to the promptings of the Spirit.

- Fears that pressing on like good stewards and maintaining our sponsorship, albeit in new structures and relationships, will be hard in the face of harsh market forces which often feel like a long, dark night.

Our fears are real. They are well founded. When we center ourselves, our fears are quieted; we know what we must tell the next generation. The journey is long. It is often hard. It will be costly, but we can make it together.

We can tell the next generation that we are companions on the journey—that we travel, women and men, religious and laity, graced by a God whose frequent message is "Be not afraid..." We can tell the next generation that it is better to die trying to be faithful than to live looking for a safe harbor, and to choose security is often to choose death. We can tell the next generation that we need them and that we want them to join us. We can tell them we know that together we will grow more secure in our evolving role as sponsors. We can tell them what the poet Rilke said:

> . . . to be patient toward all
> that is unsolved in your heart
> and to try to love the questions themselves . . . .
> Do not now seek the answers,
> which cannot be given to you
> because you would not be able to live them.
> And the point is, to live everything.
> Live the questions now.
> Perhaps you will then gradually, without noticing it,
> live along some distant day into the answer.[22]

The next generation is waiting.

Part IV

Questions for Personal
or
Group Reflection

- How have I/we shared our vision of Church? Of sponsorship? Of the evolution of the ministry?

- Who are the next generation of sponsors for our organizations? Can we name the competencies they will be required to have? Have we plans for the identification, formation and mentoring of this new generation?

- How skilled am I/are we in theological reflection and discernment? How has the congregation shared these skills with its collaborators in ministry and governance?

- What are my/our fears about the future of sponsorship? How can we address these fears?

Authors

Mary Kathryn Grant

Mary Kathryn Grant, PhD, serves as executive vice president for sponsorship and mission at the Holy Cross Health System where she has been since 1990. Her professional experience embraces both Catholic higher education and Catholic healthcare. Throughout her professional life she has focused on mission and sponsorship, mission integration, and leadership formation about which she has written, lectured, and consulted extensively.

Sister Patricia Vandenberg, CSC

Sister Patricia Vandenberg, CSC, is currently president and chief executive officer of the Holy Cross Health System, a position she has held since 1989. Her principal passion has been guiding reflections and exerting leadership to bring mission to the marketplace, spirituality to the workplace, and mission discernment to strategic planning. She has served in various healthcare leadership positions in her more than twenty-five years as a Sister of the Holy Cross.

Permissions

Notes

[1] E. E. Cummings, "Introduction to New Poems (from Collected Poems)," *Complete Poems: 1904-1962 by E. E. Cummings*, ed. George J. Firmage (1966; New York: Liveright Publishing Corporation, 1991).

[2] See Marie Augusta Neal, SNDdeN, *Catholic Sisters in Transition: From the 1960s to the 1980s* (Wilmington: Michael Glazier, 1984) and Patricia Wittberg, SC, *The Rise and Fall of Catholic Religious Orders: A Social Movement Perspective* (Albany: SUNY Press, 1994).

[3] Sister Concilia Moran, RSM, "Sponsorship: The Uneasy Question," *Hospital Progress,* October 1978: 53.

[4] Moran, "Sponsorship," 53.

[5] As quoted in *Health Progress,* September 1985: 50.

[6] A much earlier version of this text appeared in "The Enemy Within: Sponsorship After Vatican II," *Health Progress,* September 1985: 45-53.

[7] For an excellent discussion of the development and growth of the voluntary hospital system in the United States, see Patricia Tavidian, *Voluntarism in American Healthcare: Our Legacy and Our Future* (Farmington Hills: Sisters of Mercy Health Corporation, 1984).

[8] "Decree on the Up-to-Date Renewal of Religious Life," *Vatican Council II: The Conciliar and Post Conciliar Documents*, ed. Austin Flannery (Boston: St. Paul Editions, 1975).

[9] This organizational theory has been described by Lawrence E. Greiner, "Evolution and Revolution as Organizations Grow," *Harvard Business Review,* July-August 1972: 37-46, and is applied to religious congregations in an article by Lawrence Cada et al., "The Life Cycle of a Religious Community: A Sociological Model," in *Shaping the Coming Age of Religious Life* (New York: Seabury Press, 1979).

[10] R. Taguiri and J. A. Davis, "Bivalent Attributes of the Family Firm," working paper, Harvard Business School, Cambridge, Mass. Reprinted 1996, *Family Business Review II* (4): 329-39.

[11] Manfred F. R. Kets de Vries, *Family Business: Human Dilemmas in the Family Firm* (London: International Thomson Business Press, 1996) 64-65.

[12] From an unpublished study on "Transfer of Sponsorship," 1986.

[13] William Bridges, *Transitions: Making Sense of Life's Changes* (Reading: Addison-Wesley, 1980). See also James W. Fowler, *Faithful Change: The Personal and Public Challenges of Postmodern Life* (Nashville: Abingdon Press, 1996).

[14] Jon Hassler, *North of Hope* (New York: Ballantine Books, 1990) 428.

[15] Alla Bozarth-Campbell, *Life is Goodbye, Life is Hello: Grieving Well through All Kinds of Loss* (Minneapolis: CompCare Publications, 1985).

[16] David J. Nygren, CM, and Miriam D. Ukeritis, CSJ, *The Future of Religious Orders in the United States: Transformation and Commitment* (Westport: Praeger, 1993).

[17] John P. Beal, "Catholic Hospitals: How Catholic Will They Be?" *Concilium* (1994/5): 81-90.

[18] An earlier version of this treatment of change appeared in *Health Progress,* July-August 1992: 76, 79.

[19] David C. McClelland, "Introduction" and "Definition of a 'Competency'," in Lyle M. Spencer and Signe Spencer, *Competence at Work: Models for Superior Performance* (New York: Wiley, 1993) 3-15.

[20] Mary Kathryn Grant, "Sponsorship in Evolution," *Health Progress,* September 1990: 40-43.

[21] For a fuller discussion of community in workplace settings see Jane Galloway Seiling, *The Membership Organization: Achieving Top Performance through the New Workplace Community* (Palo Alto: Davies-Black Publishers, 1997).

[22] Rainer Marie Rilke, *Letters to a Young Poet*, trans. M.D. Norton (New York: W. W. Norton & Company, Inc., 1962) 35.

Resources

Beal, John P. "Catholic Hospitals: How Catholic Will They Be?" *Concilium*. 1994/5: 81-90.

Bradach, Jefferey L. *Franchise Organizations*. Cambridge: Harvard UP, 1998.

Bozarth, Alla Renee. *A Journey through Grief*. Center City: Hazelden Foundation, 1990.

Bozarth-Campbell, Alla. *Life is Goodbye, Life is Hello: Grieving Well through All Kinds of Loss*. Minneapolis: CompCare Publications, 1985.

Bridges, William. *Transitions: Making Sense of Life's Changes*. Reading: Addison-Wesley, 1980.

Burghardt, Walter J., SJ. *Tell the Next Generation: Homilies and Near Homilies*. New York: Paulist Press, 1980.

Cada, Lawrence. "The Life Cycle of a Religious Community: A Sociological Model." *Shaping the Coming Age of Religious Life*. New York: Seabury Press, 1979.

Chittister, Joan, OSB. *The Fire in These Ashes: A Spirituality of Contemporary Religious Life*. Kansas City: Sheed and Ward, 1995.

Fiand, Barbara, SNDdeN. *Wrestling with God: Religious Life in Search of Its Soul*. New York: Crossroad Publishing, 1996.

Gersick, Kelin E., et al. *Generation to Generation: Life Cycles of the Family Business.* Cambridge: Harvard UP, 1997.

Grant, Mary Kathryn. "Sponsorship in Evolution." *Health Progress,* July-August 1992: 40-43.

Guntzelman, Joan. *Blessed Grieving: Reflections on Life's Losses.* Winona: St. Mary's Press, Christian Brothers Publications, 1994.

Hassler, Jon. *North of Hope.* New York: Ballantine Books, 1990.

Kets de Vries, Manfred F. R. *Family Business: Human Dilemmas in the Family Firm.* London: International Thomson Business Press, 1996.

Kübler-Ross, Elisabeth. *On Death and Dying.* New York: Macmillan, 1969.

Moran, Sister Concilia, RSM. "Sponsorship: The Uneasy Question." *Hospital Progress,* October 1978: 53f.

Nygren, David J., CM, and Miriam D. Ukeritis, CSJ. *The Future of Religious Orders in the U.S.: Transformation and Commitment.* Westport: Praeger, 1993.

Peters, Tom. *Thriving on Chaos: Handbook for a Management Revolution.* New York: Harper Perennial, 1991.

Schein, Edgar H. *Organizational Culture and Leadership.* 2nd ed. San Francisco: Jossey-Bass, Inc., 1997.

Segundo, Juan Luis, SJ. *The Community Called Church: A Theology for Artisans of a New Humanity.* Maryknoll: Orbis Books, 1973. Vol. 1.

Seiling, Jane Galloway. *The Membership Organization: Achieving Top Performance through the New Workplace Community*. Palo Alto: Davies-Black Publishers, 1997.

Spencer, Lyle M. and Signe Spencer. *Competence at Work: Models for Superior Performance*. New York: Wiley, 1993.

Viorst, Judith. *Necessary Losses: The Loves, Illusions, Dependencies and Impossible Expectations That All of Us Have to Give Up in Order to Grow*. New York: Ballantine Books, 1986.

Watzlawick, Paul, John H. Weakland and Richard Fisch. *Change: Principles of Problem Formation and Problem Resolution*. New York: W. W. Norton & Company, Inc., 1974.

Whitehead, James D. and Evelyn Eaton Whitehead. *Shadows of the Heart: A Spirituality of the Negative Emotions*. New York: The Crossroad Publishing Company, 1995.